BEING CATHOLIC TODAY

Being Catholic Today
Your Personal Guide

*With questions for reflection or discussion
and action ideas*

BERT GHEZZI

CHARIS

SERVANT PUBLICATIONS
ANN ARBOR, MICHIGAN

Charis Books is an imprint of Servant Publications especially designed to serve Roman Catholics.

Unless otherwise noted, all Scripture quotations are from the Revised Standard Version of the Bible, © 1946, 1952, 1971 by the Division of Christian Education of the National Council of Churches of Christ in the USA. Used by permission. All rights reserved. Scripture quotations (NAB) are taken from the *New American Bible,* copyright 1991, 1986, 1970 by the Confraternity of Christian Doctrine, Washington, D.C. Used with permission. All rights reserved. No part of the *New American Bible* may be reproduced in any form without permission in writing from the copyright owner. Scripture quotations marked (NLT) are taken from the Holy Bible, New Living Translation, © 1996. Used by permission of Tyndale House Publishers, Inc., Wheaton, Illinois 60189. All rights reserved.

Permission to reproduce copyrighted material from *50 Ways to Tap the Power of the Sacraments* and *Love That Never Ends* was extended by Our Sunday Visitor, 200 Noll Plaza, Huntington, IN 46750, 1-800-348-2440. No other use of these pages is authorized.

Excerpts were taken from *Catholic and Christian* by Alan Schreck, copyright 1984 by Alan Schreck. Published by Servant Publications, Box 8617, Ann Arbor, MI 48107. Used by permission.

Excerpts were adapted from *At Home with the Sacraments: Reconciliation* by Peg Bowman, copyright 1991, 1993, 1995 by Peg Bowman. Used by permission of Twenty-Third Publications, P.O. Box 180, Mystic, CT 06355. 1-800-321-0411.

Excerpts were taken from *Hearts Aflame* by Alan Schreck, copyright 1995 by Alan Schreck. Published by Servant Publications, Box 8617, Ann Arbor, MI 48107. Used by permission.

Lyrics for "Look Beyond" by Darryl Ducote; copyright 1969 by Damean Music. Used by permission of G.I.A. Publications, Inc., exclusive agent. All rights reserved.

Adapted excerpts from *Opening to God* by Thomas H. Green, S.J., copyright 1977 by Ave Maria Press, Notre Dame, IN 46556. Used by permission of publisher.

Excerpts were taken from *Reading Scripture as the Word of God,* by George Martin, copyright 1993 by George Martin. Published by Servant Publications, Box 8617, Ann Arbor, MI 48107. Used by permission.

Excerpts from the English translation of *Rite of Penance,* copyright 1974, International Committee on English in the Liturgy, Inc. (ICEL); excerpts from the English translation of *Rite of Confirmation,* Second Edition, copyright 1975, ICEL. All rights reserved.

Excerpts were taken from *The Commandments,* by Susan Muto and Adrian van Kaam, copyright 1996 by Susan Muto and Adrian van Kaam. Published by Servant Publications, Box 8617, Ann Arbor, MI 48107. Used by permission.

"Veni Sancte Spiritus," tr. By Rev. Dr. John Webster Grant; copyright 1971 by John Webster Grant. Used by permission. All rights reserved.

Published by Servant Publications, P.O. Box 8617, Ann Arbor, Michigan 48107

Cover design: Left Coast Design, Inc., Portland, OR
Cover photograph: © Bill Varie, Westlight. Used by permission.

98 99 00 01 10 9 8 7 6 5 4 3 2 1

Printed in the United States of America
ISBN 1-56955-010-7

LIBRARY OF CONGRESS CATALOGING-IN-PUBLICATION DATA

Ghezzi, Bert.
    Being Catholic today : your personal guide : with questions for reflection or discussion and action ideas / Bert Ghezzi.
      p.   cm.
    Includes bibliographical references.
    ISBN 1-56955-010-7 (alk. paper)
    1. Christian life—Catholic authors.   2. Catholic Church—Doctrines. I. Title.
BX2350.2.G475 1998
248.4.'82—dc21   97-541475   CIP

Acknowledgments

Thanks to two editor friends whose persistent questions made this a better book: To Deacon Henry Libersat, editor of *The Florida Catholic,* who screened out some of my theological errors. And to Heidi Hess, my colleague at Servant Publications, who had the guts to challenge her boss' thoughts and to correct his prose. Any leftover mistakes are all mine.

Also by Bert Ghezzi

~

Miracles of the Saints

*Guiltless Catholic Parenting from A to Υ**

50 Ways to Tap the Power of the Sacraments

Keeping Your Kids Catholic

Sharing Your Faith

The Angry Christian

Facing Your Feelings

Contents

Foreword

Today books about the Catholic faith abound. Publishers are rushing them to press, and bookstore shelves are bursting with them. A main cause of this healthy phenomenon was the publication in 1994 of the *Catechism of the Catholic Church,* the first universal catechism in four hundred years. Its appearance opened a floodgate for books of importance to Catholics and to anyone curious about the Church.

The great majority of these books are about what Catholics believe. You can choose from hundreds of books about Catholic doctrine, the creed, theology, apologetics, liturgy, sacraments, morality, social justice, prayer and so on. There are books for the clergy, religious professionals and lay people, for the married and single, for the elderly and middle-aged and for youth and children. You name it and, armed with the right 800 phone number or address on the internet, you can have it. This flood of theological books is a great blessing. We must know as much as we can about what we *believe* because what we think shapes what we *do.* And what we do is the real test of our Christianity. Jesus set it up that way when he founded the Church.

Only a few of these books, however, are about what Catholics do. Someone wondering about how to put the Catholic faith into practice will not find many books on the subject. The best ones seem to be written by people named "Mitch." I am thinking of Mitch Finley's *The Joy of Being Catholic* and Mitch Pacwa's *Father, Forgive Me, for I Am Frustrated.* Of the others that are available, some of the more popular ones are not really practical. Recently, for example, I picked up a best-seller that promised to explain what Catholics do, only to find it more exotic than helpful.

So I detect a big need for practical instruction on being Catholic, and that's why I wrote this book. *Being Catholic Today* describes the practices that should structure a Catholic's daily life. Thus, it is a book for every Catholic or for anyone who would like to become Catholic. It will serve everyone in your pew at church, no matter how different. The lovely elderly lady in the funky straw hat praying her rosary; the middle-aged, balding man who sings too loud; or the young professional woman helping her four-year-old follow his colorful missal.

A cradle Catholic can read *Being Catholic Today* as a refresher course. A novice can use it as a handbook for getting up to speed. Participants in the Rite of Christian Initiation for Adults (RCIA) will find it especially useful. A Catholic who is confused about what he must do can consult it as a way of filling up his Catholic gaps. Even people who disagree vigorously over critical issues should find *Being Catholic Today* one of the things they agree about because it sticks to the very core of Catholic practices that we all share.

I designed *Being Catholic Today* for individual or group use. Each chapter concludes with questions for personal reflection or discussion with others. You will find action ideas designed to prompt you to put your faith into practice. Scattered throughout are quotes from Church documents and good books which are intended to whet your appetite for more good reading. You will find short lists of recommended books at the end of each chapter under the rubric "Read Me!"

Being Catholic Today is a primer. It is only a first word—and by no means the last word—on putting the Catholic faith into practice. It's like your first arithmetic book, which did not pretend to cover all of mathematics. But it was a good start and got you on your way to algebra, geometry and beyond. That's the kind of hope I have for this book. May it be a jump start for new Catholics, and a fresh start for the rest of us.

Being Catholic

"When we declare ourselves Catholic, we are not merely expressing a 'religious preference,' as we are sometimes asked to do on a hospital application. Nor are we just saying that we attend a Catholic parish on Sunday mornings, although that is certainly part of it. So what does it really mean to say, 'I'm a Catholic'?"

ONE

What Does It Mean to Be "Catholic"?

"What does being 'Catholic' mean to you?" Recently, I asked this question of Catholics of different ages and backgrounds. Here are some of the answers I got:

- "It means belonging to a church, a community that places a high emphasis on a sacramental system and responsibility to the poor, sick and hurting."

- "Being Catholic means being a part of the Bride of Christ! Christ loved his bride so much that he gave everything for her."

- "To me being Catholic means doing the right thing, standing for principles like being against abortions."

- "It's about being part of the Catholic Church, with all of its tradition and history."

- "Being Catholic is to be a privileged guest at the greatest banquet, where I am fed with both God's Word and his Body and Blood."

- "It's about embracing the beliefs of the Church, which do not change with its leaders. Regardless of who is the pastor, the basic beliefs stay the same."

- "Believing what the Bible and the Church say about God, and doing one's best to serve him."

Interesting answers, all of them. None of them are wrong because the question is subjective: "What does being 'Catholic' mean to *you?*" These are good responses, and each articulates important elements of being Catholic. However, none of them hits the nail on the head.

What do you think? What does it mean to be "Catholic"? What does it mean to call the Church "Catholic" and to describe ourselves as "Catholics"? If we want to live as good and happy Catholics, we must at least understand what it means. Right? Let's explore these questions together.

The Bible reports that it was at Antioch that the followers of Jesus were first called "Christians" (see Acts 11:26). But nowhere does Scripture refer to Christ's disciples as "Catholics." Where does that name come from?

At root, *catholic* with a small *c* means "universal." So the word *catholic* denotes something that is present everywhere or in all things. Coincidentally, the city of Antioch was also connected with the first recorded use of *catholic* to designate the Church. In A.D. 110, Ignatius, the bishop of Antioch, was martyred by wild animals in the arena at Rome. On his way to the arena, he wrote to the Christians at Smyrna, saying, "Where Christ Jesus is, there is the catholic church" (see box).

What does it mean, then, that the Church is catholic or universal? The *Catechism of the Catholic Church* (#830) says that the Church is universal in two senses. St. Ignatius summed up the first sense: Christ's presence causes the Church to be universal because Jesus, the Lord of the universe, founded it and lives in it. Thus, we are not speaking here of geographical extent. The One who is present everywhere, who keeps everything in existence, and in whom the fullness of God dwells—Christ himself—makes the Church "catholic" (see Col 1:17-19).

Secondly, the *Catechism* (#831) says the Church is universal because Christ gave it an unlimited mission. It is the *Catholic* Church because Jesus assigned it the responsibility to proclaim the good news to all people and make disciples of all nations (see

---

WHERE THE CATHOLIC CHURCH GOT ITS NAME

The first recorded use of the term "catholic church" is in a letter that Bishop Ignatius of Antioch wrote to the church at Smyrna shortly before his martyrdom in A.D. 110. Ignatius wrote, "Where the bishop is present, there let the congregation gather, just as where Jesus Christ is, there is the catholic church." For Ignatius, "catholic" church simply meant "the whole church" or "the universal church."

However, the phrase "catholic church" acquired a different meaning in the second and third centuries. Some Christians became convinced that the "universal church" led by the recognized bishops was not the true church of Jesus Christ. Some of them broke away and started their own churches.

The bishops of the "original" church of Jesus Christ distinguished themselves by calling their church the "catholic church." "Catholic" no longer meant the "total church" because not everyone who claimed to be Christian belonged to the Catholic Church.

Adapted from Alan Schreck, *Catholic and Christian* (Servant Publications: 734-677-6490), 58–59.

Mk 16:15 and Mt 28:19). "When Our Lord established the Church," wrote apologist Frank Sheed, "it consisted of one hundred and twenty Jews; it had no age at all; its teaching had not begun. And in that instant it was the *Catholic* Church. For it had been made by the universal Teacher and Lifegiver for all human beings. *That* is the inner reality...."[1] No mere human institution is anywhere near so inclusive as this divinely established one.

These truths about the universality of the Church have very practical implications for you and me. They help us get past superficial understandings of what it means to be a Catholic. When we declare ourselves Catholic, we are not merely expressing a "religious preference," as we are sometimes asked to do on a hospital application. Nor are we just saying that we attend a Catholic parish on Sunday mornings, although that is certainly part of it. So what does it really mean to say, "I'm a Catholic"?

As the Church is catholic because Christ lives in it and unites it, we are Catholics because of our relationship to him. Jesus made us members of the Church by linking us to himself, something like grafting branches onto a vine. That, in fact, is the image Jesus himself used to depict our union with him. When he said, "I am the vine, you are the branches," he was painting a word picture of our membership in the Church (see Jn 15:5). Just as a branch belongs to the vine, so we belong to Jesus. Branches get their "vine" life from the vine, and we get our "Christian" life from Christ. Like branches that wither when cut from a vine, we have no Christian life apart from him. Thus, by saying we are Catholics we acknowledge that we are one with Christ. We affirm that the Lord of the universe has made us his own.

Simply put, a Catholic is a Christian.

We share many beliefs and practices with other Christians—

with mainline Protestants, Orthodox, Evangelicals and Pentecostals. But we diverge on many others. Among the differences that separate us from other Christians, perhaps the most significant is the Catholic teaching about the Church itself. We believe that the Catholic Church is the direct descendant of that visible society which Jesus founded and handed over to Peter and the apostles to care for, propagate and govern. Vatican Council II declared authoritatively that "this Church, constituted and organized in the world as a society, subsists in the Catholic Church, which is governed by the successor of Peter [the bishop of Rome, the pope] and by the bishops in communion with him..." (see box).

THE CHURCH CHRIST FOUNDED

This is the one Church of Christ which in the Creed is professed as one, holy, catholic and apostolic; which our Savior, after His Resurrection, commissioned Peter to shepherd, and him and the other Apostles to extend and direct with authority; [and] which he erected for all ages as "the pillar and bulwark of the truth" (1 Tm 3:15). This Church, constituted and organized in the world as a society, subsists in the Catholic Church, which is governed by the successor of Peter and by the bishops in communion with him, although many elements of sanctification and of truth can be found outside of its visible structure.

Vatican Council II, *Dogmatic Constitution on the Church [Lumen Gentium]*, 8.

Above we discussed how Christ's presence and the gospel mission cause the Church to be catholic. That was the "grace" side of the story. Now with the mention of government, we have turned to look at the "law" side, which will round out our understanding of what it means to be Catholic. A Catholic is a Christian who meets certain requirements. These conditions are summed up in St. Robert Bellarmine's classic definition of the Catholic Church. He said it is "the community of men and women linked together by the profession of the same Christian faith, united in the communion of the same sacraments, under the government of the legitimate pastors and especially the one vicar of Christ on earth, the Roman pontiff."[2]

WHO IS A CATHOLIC?

They are fully incorporated into the society of the Church who, possessing the Spirit of Christ, accept her entire system and all the means of salvation given to her, and are united with her as part of her visible bodily structure and through her with Christ, who rules her through the Supreme Pontiff and the bishops. The bonds which bind men to the Church in a visible way are profession of faith, the sacraments, and ecclesiastical government and communion.

Vatican Council II, *Dogmatic Constitution on the Church [Lumen Gentium]*, 14.

Catholics are joined to Christ and to each other in the Church by these bonds: profession of faith, participation in the sacraments and submission to authority. First, we must profess the Christian faith, which is set forth in the Creed (see box), and we must believe Catholic doctrine. Second, we must receive the sacraments, which are our sources of Christian life. We must also continue to participate in them, especially the Eucharist, in order to maintain our communion with the Church. Finally, we must submit to the authority of the pope and bishops, which they normally exercise in giving teaching and pastoral direction.

THE APOSTLES' CREED

I believe in God, the Father almighty,
creator of heaven and earth.
I believe in Jesus Christ, his only son, our Lord.
He was conceived by the power of the Holy Spirit
and born of the Virgin Mary.
He suffered under Pontius Pilate,
was crucified, died and was buried.
He descended to the dead.
On the third day he rose again.
He ascended into heaven,
and is seated at the right hand of the Father.
He will come again to judge the living and the dead.
I believe in the Holy Spirit,
the holy catholic Church,
the communion of saints,
the forgiveness of sins,
the resurrection of the body,
and the life everlasting. Amen.

Sometimes we chafe at requirements, finding them restrictive or oppressive. However, our view of these three conditions for being Catholic must be quite the opposite. For they are really avenues that lead to Christ. For example, the pope and bishops are empowered to ensure that Catholic teaching does not stray from the deposit of faith that we received from Jesus.[3] This divinely appointed guarantee that the Church will remain faithful to the mind of Christ is a great protection and blessing for all Catholics.

Let me tell you about the experience of my friend Carl that illustrates what it means to be a Catholic. This true story shows how the presence of Christ in the Church—the grace side—draws a person to profess faith in and submit to the community he founded—the law side.

Carl was a college student who lived with our family for several years. He had been raised in a Christian home, but his rebellious adolescence had diluted his commitment. Carl involved himself fully in our life, sharing meals, prayer times and family events. At one point he began worshiping at Mass with us.

After several months of attending Sunday liturgies, Carl announced that he wanted to join the Catholic Church. I suggested that he might want to consider returning to the denomination he grew up in. But Carl was sure that he wanted to become a Catholic because somehow he felt irresistibly drawn to Jesus in the Eucharist. The grace side at work.

So Carl went through the process of joining the Church. He enrolled in the inquirers' classes where he learned all about life in Christ, the sacraments, the Church's government, laws, practices and so on. As he had been baptized as a baby, when he had completed his catechetical course, he made a simple profession of faith and was received into the Catholic Church. The law side at work.

I won't forget the look on Carl's face when he received his First Communion. This young man, who a few years before had been a rambunctious hellion, glowed with the innocence of a seven-year-old! These events occurred more than twenty-five years ago, but Carl, now married and the father of six, is living a faithful Catholic life and enjoying it more.

What attracted Carl to the Catholic Church was the reality that makes it universal—the dynamic love of God generously expressed in a frail, human community. In a fairly ordinary parish, Carl encountered the Real Presence of Jesus which worked on him like a spiritual magnet. Then he came to profess faith in the community that Jesus founded and entrusted to the apostles and their successors to lead.

Maybe up until now your experience as a Catholic does not match Carl's. You may have set your sights too low. Perhaps considering what it really means to be Catholic will help you elevate your view and enlarge your experience of God. "Look beyond the bread you eat," declares a popular liturgical song, "and see your Savior and your Lord."[4]

FOR REFLECTION AND DISCUSSION

1. What is the root meaning of the word *catholic*?

2. How does the presence of Christ cause the Church to be catholic?

3. How does the mission to spread the gospel make the Church catholic?

4. What does it mean to you to be Catholic?

5. What three requirements bind Catholics to Christ and the Church? In what sense are they life-giving?

ACTION IDEAS

1. For the next month, pray the Apostles' Creed once each day. Pray it reflectively, affirming your belief in each of its phrases.

2. Enhance your understanding of the Church by studying the following Scripture texts: John 15:1-17; Acts 2:42-47, 4:32-37. Ask these questions: What was the original writer saying? What does the text say to you today?

3. Read about the Church in either the *Catechism of the Catholic Church* (#748–870), or the *Dogmatic Constitution on the Church* (1–42). Ask yourself what was the most significant thing you learned in your reading and what you might do differently to be more faithfully or effectively Catholic.

READ ME!

- *Catechism of the Catholic Church* (#748–870).

- Vatican Council II, *Dogmatic Constitution on the Church [Lumen Gentium]* (Pauline Books & Media: 800-876-4463) is the authoritative Catholic teaching on the Church.

- Alan Schreck, *Catholic & Christian* (Servant Publications: 734-677-6490) is a good introduction to the distinctive elements of the Catholic faith.

When Catholics Come of Age

O n Christmas Eve, 1224, St. Francis of Assisi gave his friends at Greccio, Italy, a great surprise. When the villagers arrived for midnight Mass, outside the church they found the first crèche. An ox and an ass hovered over a straw-filled manger that awaited the arrival of the Christ child. Awestruck, the tiny congregation celebrated Mass at the stable scene, imagining, I suppose, that they had been transported back in time to Bethlehem. St. Francis, the deacon, chanted the gospel. "For to you," he sang, "is born this day in the city of David a Savior, who is Christ the Lord. And this will be a sign for you: you will find a babe wrapped in swaddling cloths and lying in a manger" (Lk 2:11-12). Then the saint preached tenderly about the infant Jesus.

Over the centuries the crèche has become the universal center-piece of the Christmas celebration. I doubt that any modern advertiser has achieved the worldwide penetration that St. Francis' dramatic innovation has won. At Christmastime people everywhere encounter the crèche and cannot ignore its plain, unambiguous announcement: God himself has come to us as a baby!

This Incarnation—the Word becoming flesh, as John says (see Jn 1:14)—is the core truth of the Catholic faith. That God became man in Christ is the central Christian mystery. In other world religions the believer must pursue the divine, always the seeker and perhaps never the finder. But for us it's the other way around. God is the hunter and we are the hunted. "In Jesus

Christ," says Pope John Paul II, "God not only speaks to man but also seeks him out. The Incarnation of the Son of God attests that God goes in search of man."[1]

Before God created time, matter and space, we were already twinkles in his eye. He yearned to have us as his own daughters and sons. Ultimately, the Father accomplished his marvelous plan by sending his Son to earth to round us up and to arrange for our adoption into the divine family. And unlike human adoption, God's making us his children is not a legal fiction. He really begets us as sons and daughters by sending us the Holy Spirit. To all who put their faith in Jesus, says John, "he gave power to become children of God," who were born not by a human decision, "but of God" (see Jn 1:12-13).

Baptism is the means God uses to birth us into his family. Some of us receive this sacrament as adults, but most of us were baptized as babies. On that pivotal day in our lives, our parents and godparents acted on our behalf. They put faith in Christ for us so that we could receive the Holy Spirit and be incorporated into the Church. They were our proxies, standing in for us until we were ready to make our own faith choices. For as adults, choose we must. As theologian Fr. Edward O'Connor says, "One baptized in infancy still has to take a personal stand for or against Christ when he comes of age."[2]

Thus, the Incarnation is no mere theological concept. It is a personal reality, the most important thing in our lives. The truth of the Incarnation is this: God is coming after us, hunting us down even if we try to run and hide from him, covering our tracks as we go. Mind-boggling, isn't it? You and I are two people among six billion humans on the planet. Don't we feel insignificant, like the psalmist who wondered why God should even think of him (see Ps 8:5)? Yet, uncannily, we are not only first in God's thoughts, but he has already sent his Son as a human being to chase us down and bring us to him. The Creator of the universe wants an intimate, personal relationship with me and you.

However, God does not force himself on us. He wants us to respond to his overtures, but he wants us to choose freely to live as his sons and daughters. So, what's involved in making an adult faith commitment? What must we do to receive the personal family relationship God extends to us?

No two people become adult Christians in exactly the same way. But we can look at some common elements in the process. These are faith, conversion and discipleship.

(1) A common initial response to the Lord's patient advances is declaring our faith. At some point we must profess our faith in Christ and in the Church he founded. We must declare in word and deed—to the Lord, to ourselves and to others—that we believe in Jesus. In everything he said about himself. In everything he did.

We may make our profession of faith in a myriad of ways: suddenly or gradually, spontaneously or formally, prompted by a great blessing or a terrible tragedy. We may wake up one day realizing that we believe in Jesus, and tell him so. We may declare our faith privately. While walking along a favorite path, for example. Or we may take our stand for Christ and the Church publicly. In the presence of the whole local parish, for example, as part of the RCIA process. In whatever manner we choose, our declaration of faith engages us with the Lord. It enables us to participate more fully in the family relationship God initiated when he made us sons and daughters through baptism.

(2) Another element in our response to God is conversion,

which we may undertake before, after or simultaneously with our profession of faith.

Conversion means a "turning." For Christians it's a dual turning —a turning our back on wrongdoing and a turning our face to the Lord (see Acts 3:19). These two movements go hand in hand, but either may precede the other. Sometimes we give ourselves to God and learn later that obedience to the Lord means recognizing a certain behavior as sin and stopping it. Or we may break with an evil pattern before we give ourselves entirely to God. For example, Carl, whom you met in the first chapter, broke with his bad companions and dissolute actions six months before he turned his life over to God. However, his friend Max gave himself to God and then one day at prayer discovered a short list of sins he needed to leave behind.

(3) Faith and conversion are the foundations for discipleship. *Discipleship* comes from a root that means "to learn," and for Christians the word means learning from Christ how to live our daily lives. Disciples yearn to model their lives on Jesus as much as possible. And discipleship is the process of receiving Christ's teaching and applying it so that we become more like him every day.

Discipleship, like faith and conversion, involves our freely making a choice. "If anyone wishes to come after me," Jesus said, "he must deny himself and take up his cross daily and follow me" (Lk 9:23, NAB). This is Christ's invitation to all who believe in him. And he wants us to say, "Yes, Lord, I will follow you. I will do whatever you want."

Faith, conversion and discipleship are not only decisions. They are continuing activities. Now and then we must renew our faith, in the midst of a family disaster, for example, or during a time when God seems more distant from us than the stars. Or we must continue our conversion by turning back to God after falling into some sin. And discipleship is the lifelong process of patterning our lives on Christ.

Jesus became one of us to show us how to live as Christians. His splendid example is another practical consequence of the Incarnation. When he invited us to link up with him and go his way, he assured us that with his grace we could do it: "Take my yoke upon you and learn from me, for I am meek and humble of heart; and you will find rest for yourselves. For my yoke is easy, and my burden light" (Mt 11:29-30, NAB).

FALL IN LOVE WITH JESUS CHRIST

Let yourselves be charmed by Christ, the Infinite who appeared among you in visible and imitable form. Let yourselves be attracted by his example, which has changed the history of the world and directed it toward an exhilarating goal. Let yourselves be loved by the love of the Holy Spirit, who wishes to turn you away from worldly things to begin in you the life of the new self, created in God's way in righteousness and true holiness.

Fall in love with Jesus Christ, to live his very life, so that our world may have life in the light of the gospel.

Pope John Paul II, "Message for the Annual World Day of Prayer for Vocations," *The Pope Speaks* 37, no.3; (May–June 1992): 131.

FOR REFLECTION AND DISCUSSION

1. In what main way does Christianity differ from other world religions?

2. What does the Incarnation mean to me? What practical consequences does it have for me?

3. What does it mean for a person to become a daughter or son of God?

4. How have I responded to God's initiatives to make me a member of his divine family?

5. What does it mean to make a profession of faith? What does declaring my faith do for my relationship with God?

6. What does conversion mean? Why is conversion an important element in my response to God?

7. What is discipleship? What must I do to become a disciple of Christ?

ACTION IDEAS

1. For the next month set aside an hour each week to think about your relationship with God. You may prefer to take two half-hour blocks. Ask yourself questions like these: How have I experienced God's action in my life? How have I responded to God? Have I ever run from him? What is the status of my faith? Is there something in my life that blocks my relationship with God? What can I do differently to respond more fully to God? Consider keeping track of your reflections in a notebook.

2. Undertake this exercise for growing in faith: read the Gospel of Mark in one sitting. Mark is the shortest of the Gospels, sixteen brief chapters with a total of only 678 verses. You will need two or three hours to do it. As you read, ask these questions: What is Mark saying? What is this Gospel saying to me?

3. To learn what Christ expects of you as a disciple, for the next month study the Sermon on the Mount, found in the Gospel of Matthew, chapters five through seven. Start by reading the whole sermon; then read through it slowly, perhaps a few verses each day. Consider reading and discussing it with family members or friends. Ask what these chapters were saying to the original readers of the Gospel. And ask what they are saying to you. What one thing could you do differently to follow Christ more closely?

READ ME!

- The *Catechism of the Catholic Church* (#142–97) describes our response to God.

THREE

A Catholic Is a Student for Life

Being a Catholic involves becoming a student for life. It's not nearly as formidable as it might seem. We're not talking about attending classes, writing papers or taking exams. Only Catholics who aspire to be religious professionals must do these things that most of us have happily left behind. We are talking about knowing the faith and doing what it takes to increase our knowledge.

Catholics need knowledge about many subjects. We must know about God. About his revelation in Scripture. About the teachings of Christ, which we call doctrine. About the Church and the sacraments. About God's laws and the laws of the Church. About prayer and worship, and much more. I have been a Catholic for more than half a century and think that I have a decent grasp of the basics. But I remain a lifelong student of the faith because I still have much to learn.

Catholics, however, are students for life not only because our quest for knowledge is perpetual. We also study the faith "for life" because our knowledge shapes the way we live as Christians. The more we know about God, for example, the more we can love him truly and let him love us as he wants. And the more we know of Christ's teaching, the more we can conform to the patterns of behavior he showed us. Thus, what we think about God and the Church somehow defines our experience. Knowing less may limit me. For instance, if I don't appreciate the truth that Christ died

for my sins, I may wallow perennially in my guilt and guilt feelings. But knowing more may expand my openness to God. I can
receive a deeper unity with him, for example, when I grasp that at
every Mass I am joined sacramentally with Christ in his perfect
sacrifice.

Let me make an example of myself. In the past several years I
have studied the sacraments, the saints and the Lord's Prayer (the
"Our Father"). Here are some ways the knowledge I obtained
enhanced my Christian life:

THE MESSAGE OF THE NEW CATECHISM

Looking at the way the *Catechism* is organized makes ...
fundamental truths vividly clear. *The creed, or "profession
of faith," comes first.* Why? We would have nothing to say
as Christians if the Father had not spoken through the
Son and in the Holy Spirit, calling us into communion
with them. The contents of the articles of the "Apostles'
Creed" amount in the end to a simple, but glorious affirmation: the uncreated persons of the blessed Trinity call
out in love to created persons to summon us to ultimate
communion and to enable us to enjoy this communion.

What comes next in the *Catechism* is not the commandments, as one might expect. Rather, *part two of the
Catechism presents the sacraments.* The natural human
response to hearing the affirmation of the triune God's
invitation to communion would be to want to do something about it.... The structure of the Catechism in effect
tells us that, by ourselves, we cannot respond to this

- When I studied the sacrament of reconciliation, I learned that the Church typically classifies it as a sacrament of healing. It does so because the sin of one member damages the health of the entire body of Christ. When the offending member repents and makes use of the sacrament, the body of Christ is restored to health. While this knowledge has not renewed my innocence, it has made me somewhat more resistant to wrongdoing.

- In my study of the saints I noticed that Francis of Assisi, Clare, Dominic, Teresa of Avila, Vincent Ferrer and many others

---

invitation. God himself makes it possible for us to respond through the manifold grace of the sacraments through which Christ works to conform us to himself....

Only in light of the transforming and enabling grace of Christ can we speak about *the Ten Commandments and the Beatitudes, which form the substance of part three of the Catechism.* The high moral ideals of the Christian life can be pursued and attained only through the grace of Christ who empowers us to live human life at a new, supernatural level....

Then *in part four of the Catechism,* we see an anticipation of the goal of Christian life—*easy communication and communion with the Father,* through Christ and in the Spirit. The "Our Father" captures the moment of communion between the triune God and the believer.

Adapted from J. Augustine DiNoia, O.P., and others, *The Love That Never Ends: A Key to the Catechism of the Catholic Church* (Our Sunday Visitor: 800-348-2440), 15–16.

focused their lives on Christ crucified and drew their spiritual energy from his victory on the cross. For instance, Thomas More, one of sixteenth-century England's most prominent statesmen, spent Fridays meditating on Christ's passion. The example of these saints prompted me to take time regularly to thank the Lord for his willingness to die for me.

• Unpacking the meaning of the petitions of the "Our Father" has also enriched me. For example, I heard a priest preach on "forgive us our trespasses." He asked, "What if the person we offended most was the one who would decide whether we got admitted to heaven?" That scary thought has helped me be less judgmental and more forgiving.

So, I see study as a way of giving us wider access to God and as an aid to our enjoying a richer, happier Christian life.

Since we acquire knowledge in various ways, our study can involve diverse activities. Reading may come to mind first because we normally identify books with study. In fact, for centuries the Church has encouraged us to make *lectio divina* or "spiritual reading" a daily activity. However, we have many other options for learning about the faith. We get knowledge by listening, for example, to homilies at Mass or to books and speakers via audio-cassette while we are driving. Discussions with friends and formal courses are also valuable opportunities for study. And in our electronic age, a wise use of videos and the internet may provide contemporary alternatives for *lectio divina*.

Deciding what to study is easy. We should investigate something we feel we don't know very well. Or something we are curious about. For example, maybe you are puzzled about the meaning of "redemption," the "resurrection of the body" or some other Christian reality. Perhaps you wonder why Christ established the Church, or why he chose to relate to us through sacraments. You may have questions about how to apply the Ten Commandments or the Beatitudes to your life. Or you may want to learn how to draw closer to God in prayer. Whatever gaps you see in your knowledge of the faith, study is the means for filling them. Once you begin to pursue answers, new questions will come up, igniting a chain reaction that will expand your understanding.

The place to begin our search for answers is the *Catechism of the Catholic Church*. We are perhaps the first generation ever to have such an accessible summary of the Catholic faith. It lays out the essentials of Catholic teaching in four strategically arranged parts—the creed, the sacraments, the moral life and prayer (see box on pages 34 and 35).

We may dip into the *Catechism* at any point to explore our questions. Or we might undertake to read through it systematically. In either case, we may find it helpful to consult one of the many guides that are available. The *Catechism* is not an easy read, but we will benefit significantly from putting effort into digesting its message.

Many other good summaries of the faith exist, some quite popularly written. In my view the best is *The Catholic Vision* by Edward O'Connor, C.S.C. (See Read Me! for recommended titles.)

We also have a study Aide who sets our quest for knowledge of the faith apart from other intellectual enterprises. That's the Holy Spirit, and his presence makes our reading (or listening or viewing) truly "spiritual." The Bible says the Spirit is a Helper who enlightens us and brings to mind all that God revealed in Christ (see Jn 14:26 and 16:7-15). Engaging him in our learning activities makes the job easier and much more productive. So let's link up with our divine partner and get on with being a student for life.

FOR REFLECTION AND DISCUSSION

1. Why must we become students for life?

2. In what ways does study enrich our Christian lives?

3. How has studying the faith benefited me?

4. Why is the *Catechism of the Catholic Church* such a valuable book?

5. How can I engage the Holy Spirit as a help to my study?

6. What one thing could I do differently to study the faith more effectively?

ACTION IDEAS

1. Familiarize yourself with the *Catechism of the Catholic Church*. You can buy an inexpensive paperback copy or borrow one from most libraries. Examine the contents pages, noticing the four main parts. Read Pope John Paul II's introduction and the prologue. Flip through the index at the back of the book. To get a feel for the *Catechism*, dip in anywhere your curiosity leads and read a few pages. Or as a sample read paragraphs 599–618 about Christ's death for our sins. Ask yourself how you can use this book to help you grow in faith.

2. Identify some aspect of the faith you don't know much about or would like to understand better. Study about the topic, using the *Catechism of the Catholic Church* and other books recommended in the Read Me! lists of this book. Write down the questions you have about the subject and look for answers as you read.

3. Consider building spiritual reading into your daily or weekly schedule. Consult the Read Me! lists in this book or the brief bibliography. Pick a book that interests you and buy or borrow a copy. To make room in your life for study, you will have to decide when, where and for how long you will read the book of your choice. Aim to complete the book within one month. Evaluate your experience, asking what you might do to make it better the next time. Then select another book, and do it again.

READ ME!

- The *Catechism of the Catholic Church* is available from several publishers. There are a number of resources to help you understand it better. Some of these are listed below.

Guides to the Catechism

- J. Augustine DiNoia and others, *The Love That Never Ends: A Key to the Catechism of the Catholic Church* (Our Sunday Visitor: 800-348-2440) conveys an enlightening perspective on the *Catechism*.

- John Hardon, S.J., *The Faith* (Servant Publications: 734-677-6490) is ideal for readers who like a question-and-answer approach to catechetics.

- Henry Libersat, *A Catholic Confession of Faith* (Pauline Books & Media: 800-876-4463) is a series of four inspirational pamphlets designed to help readers apply the *Catechism* to daily life.

- Alfred McBride, O. Praem., *Essentials of the Faith* (Our Sunday Visitor: 800-348-2440) is another very good guide to using the *Catechism*.

- Susan Muto and Adrian van Kaam, *The Woman's Guide to the Catechism of the Catholic Church* (Servant Publications: 734-677-6490).

Introductions to the Catholic Faith

- Mitch Finley, *The Joy of Being Catholic* (Crossroad: 212-532-3650) gives readers a "feel" for living as a Catholic.

- *Handbook for Today's Catholic* (Liguori: 314-464-2500) is a practical, short read.

- Edward O'Connor, C.S.C., *The Catholic Vision* (Our Sunday Visitor: 800-348-2440).

- Alan Schreck, *Basics of the Faith* (Servant Publications: 734-677-6490) is an easy-to-read summary of Catholic teaching.

- Frank Sheed, *Theology for Beginners* (Servant Publications: 734-677-6490) is a popular, thought-provoking classic.

Receiving Daily Graces

"We should approach the sacraments with active, aggressive faith, expecting Jesus to act in our life. 'Here I am, Lord,' we should say to him at Mass. 'I am a stationary target. Let your Spirit rush over me. I give you permission to do whatever you want to me.'"

FOUR

Bring the Sacraments to Life

Sometimes I imagine how exciting it would have been to have lived in Judea at the time of Christ. What a privilege it would have been to have heard Jesus teach in person! I would have been thrilled to have watched him heal the lame, the deaf and the blind. Perhaps I might have had a chance to speak to him face to face. I even envision what it would have been like to have witnessed his horrible death and his triumphant resurrection.

But then I also wonder how I would have reacted to some of the shocking things Jesus did and said. What would I have thought of him the day he drove the hucksters out of the temple? Would I have stayed with him when he said outrageous things like, "He who eats my flesh and drinks my blood has eternal life" (Jn 6:54)? Many disciples tripped over that claim and turned heel on him. Maybe I would have been among them.

So I emerge from my reveries glad to be a follower of Christ on the eve of the third millennium. In a real sense I am much nearer to Jesus now than I would have been two thousand years ago. Then, even if I had pushed through the crowd to brush against him, he would have only been physically present to me. Now, however, Christ is present in me spiritually. I am united to him in a bond more intimate than any mere human relationship. "If a man loves me," Jesus said, "he will keep my word, and my Father will love him, and we will come to him and make our home with him" (Jn 14:23). You can't get much more intimate than that! Thus, had I become an acquaintance of Jesus by the Sea of Galilee, he and I may have remained *two*, as I may have abandoned him long before his resurrection. But today because of what Jesus has done to me, he and I are *one*. Then I would have been *with* Christ, but now I am *in* him. Then Christ would have been *with* me, but now he is *in* me. I can hardly begin to comprehend the thought.

Just what is it that Christ has done to achieve this union with us? His mission on earth was to make it possible for us to become adopted daughters and sons of God. He was to put us in position to be incorporated into the Trinity, sharing God's own life. He accomplished his work by his death, resurrection and ascension to the Father, who then poured out the Spirit to beget his sons and daughters.

These were extraordinary events, but also remarkable were the arrangements Jesus made to continue his work of uniting men and women to God. Today we call these arrangements "sacraments." But Jesus spoke of them descriptively and personally. Consider the full text of his "hard saying" which I quoted above: "Unless you eat the flesh of the Son of man and drink his blood, you have no life in you; he who eats my flesh and drinks my blood has eternal life, and I will raise him up at the last day. For my flesh is food indeed, and my blood is drink indeed. He who eats my flesh and drinks my blood abides in me, and I in him" (Jn 6:53-56). Christ was speaking of the Eucharist, the sacrament he created the night before his death.

Jesus and the Church give us seven sacraments. The *Catechism of the Catholic Church* presents them in three groups. Baptism, confirmation and Eucharist are sacraments of initiation that unite us to God and bind us to each other in the community of believers. Two are sacraments of healing, reconciliation and the anointing of the sick. Matrimony and holy orders are sacraments that provide for the salvation of others (see box).

EMPOWERED BY THE SACRAMENTS

Each of the seven sacraments plays an important life-giving role that empowers us for everyday living. *Baptism, confirmation and the Eucharist are sacraments of initiation because they establish and maintain our union with the Lord.*

- Baptism cleanses us spiritually and plunges us into God's life, creating a Father-child relationship that will last forever.
- In confirmation, the Holy Spirit comes to us with gifts and graces—practical tools that assist us on our journey.
- The Lord nourishes our souls with life-giving food, his own body and blood, in the Eucharist.

Two social sacraments increase life in Christ.
- Matrimony provides continuous spiritual support for marriage relationships and family living, and involves couples with God in creating new human lives.
- In holy orders the Holy Spirit empowers priests with a share in Christ's mediation, enabling them to perform the sacramental actions that give and sustain our divine lives.

Two sacraments ensure our spiritual and physical health.
- Sinful and broken, we meet Jesus in the sacrament of reconciliation. There the Lord, who died for our sins, forgives us personally, as he did the woman caught in

continued on page 46

continued from page 45

adultery (see Jn 8:3-11), and heals us, as he did the man born blind (see Jn 9:1-4).

- The touch of the Spirit in the anointing of the sick brings physical and spiritual healing to us, restoring our health and preparing those near death for direct and personal union with God.

The sacraments are like power plants that generate a vast supply of supernatural energy. They make God's power available to us, and we can use as much or as little as we choose. They do their life-giving and life-sustaining work whether we're aware of it or not.

But when we approach the sacraments with little appreciation, understanding or faith, we draw much less spiritual power from them than they provide. Then we are like people who sit shivering in dark houses, not realizing that by flipping a few switches, we could turn on the heat and the lights. The slogan of a great electrical appliance company could be a banner headline on an advertisement for the sacraments: We bring good things to life! But to make that come true we must actively tap their power.

Bert Ghezzi, *50 Ways to Tap the Power of the Sacraments* (Our Sunday Visitor: 800-348-2440), 14–15.

Each of these sacraments puts us in touch with the most significant event in history—the death and resurrection of Jesus. In a mysterious way, they make it possible for us to be really present at Calvary and the empty tomb. They are transmitters that allow us to experience the power and the benefits of Christ's saving work.

At the core of each sacrament are signs that appeal to our senses. Christ wants to do things to our souls, but he knows that the only way to get to them is through our bodies. So he built the sacraments around physical symbols. Like water, bread, wine, oil, laying on of hands and words which we could feel, see, taste, smell and hear.

Here are some of the things Jesus does for us in the sacraments.

- In baptism, for example, he takes water and cleanses our souls of every stain of sin.

- Bread and wine become the Body and Blood of Christ in the Eucharist. With these he nourishes our spirits.

- He takes oil in confirmation to strengthen our inner beings, and in the anointing of the sick he applies oil to heal our souls and our bodies.

- In confirmation and holy orders, Christ uses the laying on of hands to equip us for service in the Church and the world.

- With the words spoken in matrimony, he creates a covenant between a man and a woman.

- In reconciliation he authorizes words of absolution that repair a damaged or broken relationship.

Because Jesus himself is at work in the sacraments, they can make a big difference in our lives. St. Francis Xavier, for example, once baptized an Indian woman who had been in labor three days and was about to die in childbirth. Immediately after her baptism, she delivered a healthy baby. As a result everyone in her Hindu village became a Catholic. Bishop Sheen once asked an alcoholic priest to worship at Mass daily and to spend extra time praying before the Blessed Sacrament reserved in the tabernacle. In six months the priest was sober. A man who had been unfaithful to his wife for twenty years wandered accidentally into a parish communal penance service, stayed and tearfully repented. Then he worked at repairing his damaged relationship with his wife.

Well, I'm not Francis Xavier or Bishop Sheen, you say. Yes, these are extraordinary examples. Why don't we see more of the power of the Holy Spirit busting out of the sacraments? Perhaps because Jesus normally works more quietly and subtly in our lives. That's true, I think. But at the same time I wonder if we Catholics simply don't expect very much of the sacraments. We all feel the need for spiritual strength, guidance, comfort, nourishment, healing and help of all kinds, yet I suspect we often bypass the sacraments. Sometimes I think they must be the most underutilized power sources on the planet.

What can we do to bring the sacraments to life? How can we approach Christ in the sacraments and let him do whatever he wants to us? We can take several steps.

(1) Knowing about the sacraments will enable us to find Jesus more readily in them. So we should do some studying about them (see Read Me!).

(2) We should use the sacraments more and participate in them wholeheartedly. If I stay away from the sacrament of reconciliation, for example, I may be stunting my spiritual growth.

(3) We should approach the sacraments with active, aggressive faith, expecting Jesus to act in our life. "Here I am, Lord," we should say to him at Mass. "I am a stationary target. Let your Spirit rush over me. I give you permission to do whatever you want to me."

Then watch out! Christ is sure to answer our prayer.

FOR REFLECTION AND DISCUSSION

1. Why do Christ and the Church give us sacraments? What is their primary purpose?

2. Why do you think the sacraments use physical signs?

3. What kinds of things does Christ do for us in the sacraments?

4. How have I experienced Christ in the sacraments?

5. What can I do differently to benefit more from the sacraments?

ACTION IDEAS

1. Pick one sacrament and study about it, using the *Catechism of the Catholic Church.* You may want to consult commentaries on the *Catechism* and other books. At the end of your study, ask, What is the most important thing have I learned? How can I apply it to my life?

2. Volunteer to be a sponsor for an adult catechumen who is seeking baptism in your parish's RCIA process. Use the experience as an opportunity to learn about baptism and to renew your own adult commitment to Christ and your baptismal vows.

3. Arrange to be present at the anointing of the sick for a relative or friend. If your parish offers a communal celebration of the sacrament, you could invite an elderly relative or neighbor to participate and take them to the event. Or you could make arrangements with the parish to have the sacrament administered at home for a sick or elderly person. Afterward, reflect on your experience.

READ ME!

- *Catechism of the Catholic Church* (#1210–1666).

- Bert Ghezzi, *50 Ways to Tap the Power of the Sacraments* (Our Sunday Visitor: 800-348-2440) is a popularly written introduction to the sacraments.

- Edward D. O'Connor, C.S.C., *The Catholic Vision* (Our Sunday Visitor: 800-348-2440), 388–411.

FIVE

What Do I Get Out of Mass?

I can empathize with my children who as teens often said they didn't "get anything" out of Mass. I went through a period in my life feeling the same way. At that time I viewed Mass attendance as an obligation. The singing was a distraction, the standing-kneeling-sitting was rigmarole, and the sermons were *bor-ring!* But somewhere along the way I discovered I was looking at it backward and I did a 180-degree turn. I stopped looking for what I could get out of Mass. Ever since, I have tried to put as much into my worship as I can. That has made all the difference.

Of course, we are supposed to get a lot out of Mass. And we do. Christ himself comes to us in his Word and in the Eucharist. He takes us to himself and gives himself to us, although we may not experience a thing. The Eucharist is a meal. We can see, smell, taste and touch the bread and wine. It really is food for our souls, the Lord himself coming to nourish us spiritually. However, because Christ works through the Eucharist whether or not we are aware of it, we can leave Mass feeling as if nothing happened.

But we can get even more out of Mass by putting more into it. If we approach the sacrament with greater understanding and faith, we receive greater spiritual benefit. Celebrating the Eucharist with awareness and expectancy allows Christ to accomplish more in us. We may even leave church realizing that something special happened to us.

Involved here is a basic principle of Christianity—the unconditional giving of self—which threads throughout the fabric of the

Catholic faith. In the Incarnation, for example, Christ became a human being, no strings attached. Although he was God, he gave up everything to join us in our humanity. On the cross, Christ gave his life for us—again, no strings attached—in a perfect sacrifice. That's also what's happening at Mass. The sacrament makes present Christ's great act of love, but with a difference. This time he gathers up you and me and includes us in his offering to the Father. That's why we get more if we give more.

What can we do differently if we want to get more out of the Mass? The answer: put our minds, our bodies, our hearts—our all—into it.

Put our minds into it. Studying the Mass will stimulate a big improvement in our experience. We should do a little selective reading to get an overview (see Read Me!). You may find it interesting to dip into these Scripture passages that tell how it all began: Luke 22:7-20; Matthew 26:17-29; Mark 14:12-25; 1 Corinthians 11:23-26. It's also helpful just to read through the order of worship in a missal, which is a book that contains all the texts used at Mass. Often the worship books in the pews of your parish church are "missalettes," and maybe you can borrow one for your study.

After you get a feel for what's happening at Mass, you might consult the *Catechism of the Catholic Church* on the liturgy and the Eucharist. Begin with paragraphs 1187–99 and 1406–19. Then slowly study your way through paragraphs 1136–86 and through paragraphs 1322–1405.

All that long-term study will give you valuable background. You will also benefit from some study right before Mass. Many Catholics, for example, prepare for worship by previewing the Scriptures that will be read at the Liturgy of the Word. Some parishes list these in the bulletin a week ahead, but for the sake of

GET READY TO WORSHIP ACTIVELY

In order that the liturgy may be able to produce its full effects, it is necessary that the faithful come to it with proper dispositions, that their minds should be attuned to their voices, and that they should cooperate with divine grace lest they receive it in vain.

* * *

Mother Church earnestly desires that all the faithful should be led to that full, conscious and active participation in liturgical celebrations which is demanded by the very nature of the liturgy. Such participation by the Christian people as a "chosen race, a royal priesthood, a holy nation, God's own people" (1 Pt 2:9; see 2:4-5), is their right and duty by reason of their baptism.

* * *

The Church ... earnestly desires that Christ's faithful, when present at this mystery of faith, should not be there as strangers or silent spectators. On the contrary, through a good understanding of the rites and prayers they should take part in the sacred action conscious of what they are doing, with devotion and full collaboration. They should be instructed by God's word and be nourished at the table of the Lord's body; they should give thanks to God; by offering the Immaculate Victim, not only through the hands of the priest, but also with him, they should learn also to offer themselves; through Christ the Mediator, they should be drawn day by day into ever more perfect union with God and with each other, so that finally God may be all in all.

Vatican Council II, *Constitution on the Sacred Liturgy [Sacrosanctum Concilium]*, 11, 14, 48.

convenience you may need to invest in a Sunday missal. Someone at your parish office or local religious bookstore can probably help you get one.

Put our bodies into it. One reason people don't get much out of Mass is passivity. They see it as a performance and themselves as viewers in an audience. They may even come to church in their "couch potato" mode, trained by watching T.V. to expect to be passively entertained. No wonder they feel that nothing is happening for them! Mass *is* a great drama, representing in word and action the saving work of Christ. But it is not merely a show put on for us by the celebrant, the choir and a few lay ministers.

If I were to compare Mass to any modern entertainment at all, I might say it is like dinner theater. You may have participated in one of these mealtime shows where a few actors involve everyone in their drama. The more the guests participate, the better the show. If the guests don't get involved, the show goes on, but without much luster or pizzazz.

Mass is something like that, but in an entirely different order. The priest has the "lead" and everyone in the congregation is a "player." Together we gather at the eucharistic meal to act out the great story of our salvation. Christ arranged it that way so all of us could share sacramentally in his act of perfect worship, offering ourselves with him to the Father. He intended us to participate as actively as we can with him in this memorial of his sacrifice.

Active participation at Mass requires that we throw our bodies into it. We sit, we stand and we kneel because our posture helps us express the right attitudes toward God. We make gestures like the sign of the cross to mark ourselves as Christ's disciples and to acknowledge receipt of blessings. We embrace or shake hands to show our love for sisters and brothers in Christ. With our ears we listen to the proclamation of Scripture and attend to the corporate prayers. With our mouths we repent of our sin, respond to God's Word, proclaim our faith, say "Amen" to our self-offering and sing God's praises. I do all these things with gusto, and I encourage you to do the same. You will get more out of Mass if you do, both spiritually and experientially.

Put our hearts into it. God became a human being in Christ to show us why he created us. He loved each of us even before we were born and wanted an intimate relationship with us. His plan was to include us as daughters and sons in his divine family, so he designed us in his image so that we would fit right in. And Christ's death and resurrection made it all possible.

Mass makes present sacramentally Christ's supreme act of love, and he draws us into the action, so that we too can express our love for God with him. Every Mass, then, is an opportunity for us to realize our purpose. Even before we fully understand all the intricacies of the liturgy, we can simply tell the Lord we love him and let him love us. What more could we want to get out of Mass?

FOR REFLECTION AND DISCUSSION

1. What am I supposed to "get" out of the Mass?

2. Why is it that I will receive more from celebrating the Eucharist if I give more of myself?

3. What one thing can I do differently to worship better at Mass?

ACTION IDEAS

1. Try this experiment. For the next three months keep a journal of what you learned from the Liturgy of the Word at Sunday Mass. Write in a notebook your answers to two questions:

(1) What does God seem to be saying to me through today's readings? (2) What would I have to do to apply this Word to my life? If you enjoy this experience, do it again.

2. Select several key parts of the liturgy which you will "throw yourself into" during the next three months at Sunday Mass. (Consider actively offering yourself with the bread and wine at the offertory; worshiping Jesus at the consecration; affirming your part in the Lord's sacrifice at the great Amen; and quietly reverencing the Lord after receiving communion.) Evaluate your effort after three months. Then do it again.

3. Invite your family or a few friends to spend five minutes after Sunday Mass discussing the one thing that struck each of you most about the day's liturgy. Agree to do this for a dozen consecutive Sundays. At the end of the period, evaluate the activity, and consider doing it over again.

4. Discuss with your pastor or his delegate the possibility of your performing some service during the liturgy, perhaps as an usher, acolyte, reader or minister of the Eucharist. If invited, make a personal commitment to perform the service faithfully.

READ ME!

- The *Catechism of the Catholic Church* (#1135–58) sums up the Church's teaching on celebrating the Mass.

- Bert Ghezzi, *50 Ways to Tap the Power of the Sacraments* (Our Sunday Visitor: 800-348-2440) is a good introduction to active worship.

- Archbishop Daniel E. Pilarczyk, *Understanding the Mass* (Our Sunday Visitor: 800-348-2440) is a brief, popular explanation of the Mass.

SIX

Living Through the Year With Christ

Recently my wife Mary Lou and I had a chance to visit with two favorite relatives, my cousin Rosemarie and her husband John. Over a wonderful meal at one of Orlando's finest restaurants, we reviewed what had happened in our families since we last met. Rosemarie and I grew up together, and as always we laughed about things we had done as kids. Over appetizers, we looked at each other's photo albums, remembering births, comings of age and deaths.

Among Rosemarie's pictures was a current photograph of Felix, a first cousin of my maternal grandmother. John had snapped it on a visit to Felix's ancestral home in Piaggine, Italy, a tiny village carved in a hillside south of Naples. Felix bore a striking resemblance to my grandma, my uncles and my mother. I thought I saw something of myself in his Mediterranean features, and something of my own kids, too. The experience made me wonder about the flow of events over the century that have brought my family from a little mountain town in Italy to the watery flatlands of central Florida.

Remembering the past is one of the activities that distinguishes us as humans. Other animals don't seem to "remember" in the way we can. Corky, my cocker spaniel, for example, can always remember where the treats are, but he cannot recall his ancestry. A friend of mine says he thinks God invented time so that everything doesn't happen all at once. That is, the Lord created time so that human beings would be able to live in the present, remembering the past and anticipating the future.

Just as we recall our individual histories, the Church also remembers the past. But it does so on a much grander scale. Every year the Church represents for us the great events of our salvation history, which culminated in Christ. The Church year begins not on January 1, but on the first Sunday of Advent, four Sundays before Christmas, and ends with the feast of Christ the King, the fifth Sunday before the next Christmas.

Week by week a wonderful story unfolds in the liturgy, an annual account of God's relentless, but gentle, love for us. The Church remembers the history of God's saving acts in three chief liturgical seasons:

- *From Advent through Christmas to the Epiphany* (the Sunday nearest January 6), the Church reminds us of the gradual unfolding of God's intention to perfect his creation by coming to dwell among us, a plan realized in the birth of Christ. It focuses us on his threefold coming: God's becoming a man in Christ, his coming to us in our daily lives, and his final coming as king and judge to wrap up history and take us home to heaven.

- *During Lent through Easter to Pentecost,* the Church recalls the main events of salvation history. At this time the liturgy concentrates on the work of Christ in his passion, death, resurrection, ascension and the sending of the Holy Spirit. The Church represents Christ's saving acts to call us to renewed faith, conversion and discipleship. This season ends with Trinity Sunday, the Sunday after Pentecost.

- *The Sundays of Ordinary Time* make up the third liturgical season. These Sundays provide the backdrop for the pivotal events we recall during the Christmas and Easter seasons. While we call the season "ordinary," we should not mistakenly conclude that it is inconsequential. In fact, it's an extraordinarily important time for us. On these Sundays we normally reflect on the life and teaching of Jesus as a way to foster our own Christian growth. The Sunday after Epiphany, which celebrates Jesus' baptism, is the first Sunday of Ordinary Time. Usually several more of these Sundays precede Lent, the number fluctuating annually depending on the date of Easter, which hops about during March and April. Ordinary Time picks up again on the second Sunday after Pentecost and extends through the summer until it climaxes in the feast of Christ the King.

Taken together, the Church calls these seasons the "liturgical year." We get the words *liturgical* and *liturgy* from a Greek root that referred to a public work performed by one citizen for the good of all. Philip B. Crosby's donation of a wellness center to the people of Winter Park, Florida, is a contemporary example of a liturgy in the ancient Greek sense. The Church has borrowed this word to describe the work Jesus did for the whole human race. So during the liturgical year we remember in a special way all the things Christ did to save us.

Note well, however, that the Church's remembrance of Christ's actions in the liturgy is very different from mere human recollections. Human memories are only ideas in our mind, but the Church's "memories" actually put us in touch with Christ and his sacrifice.

Humanly speaking when we recall the past, we cannot get back to the actual events and represent them. For example, my earliest memory of my grandmother is of a picnic celebration she held to welcome home her son, my Uncle Tony, from World War II. She served a delicious pumpkin flower soup, and I can still imagine its aroma and flavor. But I can't be present again at that picnic, grab Grandma's apron, hug Uncle Tony or slurp up the soup. I can only enjoy a shadowy memory of that event in my thoughts.

When we gather to celebrate the Mass, however, we don't merely recall Christ's sacrifice as we might any other historical event like the signing of the Declaration of Independence. Our remembrance at Mass is not just a shadowy memory or a mental exercise. God has arranged that when the Church remembers Christ and his saving actions, they become present to us—literally, via the sacraments. Thus Sunday by Sunday through the liturgical year, the Church sacramentally unites us to Jesus and his life, death and resurrection.

In the ancient world a liturgy was a public work that required the involvement of the citizenry. To return to an earlier example, Philip B. Crosby's wellness center is a liturgy that Winter Park towns-people participate in by consulting its experts and using its equipment. The same is true for the liturgical year. The Church sacramentally represents the life, death and resurrection of Jesus—his salvific work—so that we can participate in it and live in God's presence.

The Church walks us through the liturgical year to heighten our awareness that every day we are living with God. When we receive the Holy Spirit in baptism, he unites us to the Father and Son. That union with God is the heart of what it means to be Catholic, and it is the most important fact about us. So beginning with Advent, every Sunday of the Church's year presents realities and unfolds biblical themes that we are supposed to receive and apply to our lives. "Recalling thus the mysteries of redemption," said Vatican Council II, "the Church opens to the faithful the riches of her Lord's powers and merits, so that these are in some way made present for all time, and the faithful are enabled to lay hold upon them and become filled with saving grace."[1] The more we keep in mind, then, that God lives in us, the more strength we will have to love him and others. After all, isn't doing everything out of love what the Lord requires of us?

" G O ... T O   L O V E   A N D   S E R V E   T H E   L O R D "

Christ established the kingdom of God by his death and resurrection. Now through the sacraments, the Lord makes God's kingdom present in us so that we can work with him to bring God's saving justice to the world. In baptism, for example, we die with Christ to a disjointed world that is organized on principles that do not acknowledge God. We rise with him to live according to the Holy Spirit himself, who leads us to seek the restoration of all things in Christ.

The new life of baptism cuts through all differences—cultural, racial, national, economic—so that we come to the Eucharist as brothers and sisters in the Lord's family. At the sacrificial meal, we share the Body and Blood of Christ. By our participation in the liturgy, we learn to share our diverse gifts. This sharing that we receive and learn in the sacrament must not stop in the pews, for it is an instrument we must use to help establish God's justice in our society.

That truth is embodied in the word "Mass." The name we give to our worship service derives from the Latin form of the dismissal, *"Ite, missa est,"* "Go, you are dismissed." Now the celebrant dismisses us by charging us to spend ourselves in service: "Go in peace to love and serve the Lord."

Thus we are to embody the love of God we receive in the Eucharist, distributing it freely in the human community. The practice of the first Christians is a model for us (see Acts 4:34-35). As a response to their sharing God's abundance in the liturgy, they shared with each other from the abundance of their wealth.

Adapted from Bert Ghezzi, *50 Ways to Tap the Power of the Sacraments* (Our Sunday Visitor: 800-348-2440), 44–45.

During the liturgical year, then, we remember what God has done to save us. But our remembrance is not locked back in time, for the liturgy brings Christ and his graces into the present. In fact, right smack into the middle of our daily lives.

FOR REFLECTION AND DISCUSSION

1. How have I experienced the community sense of "liturgy" in my own life?

2. What does the Church "remember" during the liturgical year?

3. In what ways do I personally celebrate the liturgical seasons?

4. How can I celebrate the seasons of the Church's year more meaningfully?

5. Why should I try to apply the themes of the liturgical seasons to my life?

ACTION IDEAS

1. Make worship at Sunday Mass central. Take some time to prepare by reviewing the Scripture readings beforehand or reflecting on them afterward. Maybe do both.

2. Look for ways to apply the themes of the liturgical season to your personal life. In Advent, for example, when we reflect on God's coming to us, perhaps we should set aside a few minutes each day in prayer to welcome him in our hearts. And during Lent, maybe we could perform some daily act of kindness for a family member or friend. Preferably one that involved some self-sacrifice like getting up early or going out of our way.

3. Study about each of the liturgical seasons. You will probably find easy-to-read pamphlets and books in racks at the back of your church or in a religious bookshop.

READ ME!

- The *Catechism of the Catholic Church* discusses the liturgical year in paragraphs 1163–73.

- Bert Ghezzi, *50 Ways to Tap the Power of the Sacraments* (Our Sunday Visitor: 800-348-2440) suggests many easy ways to celebrate the liturgical year.

Opening to God

"The word *saint* derives from a Latin root that means 'holy' or 'consecrated.' In that sense, we are all saints because the Holy Spirit is in us and lets us share his holiness. His presence makes it possible for us to become more Christlike, as he alone enables our feeble wills to obey Jesus' seemingly outrageous and impossible commands, like: 'You, therefore, must be perfect, as your heavenly Father is perfect'" (Mt 5:48).

SEVEN

Spend Time With the Lord

I have decided to spoil Alex, my first grandchild. He's only one year old, so he's not yet aware of my intentions. Right now he doesn't even seem to recognize me. When I hold him he doesn't look at me much, except to grab for my glasses. Many fascinating things compete for his attention. A TV remote. A fluttering ceiling fan. A squirrel darting across the road. But I'm his grandfather and I'm persistent. Someday soon he'll notice me, and then he'll covet time with me. I'm sure of it.

Sometimes I think I relate to God the way Alex relates to me. Maybe it's the same for you, too. God, our Father, wants us to know him and love him. He comes after us, trying to get us to notice him. But a multitude of other things dominates our attention. Family, work, school, commuting, exercise, recreation, church, service—the ever-expanding busyness of life consumes us. Only rarely does God receive more than a passing glance.

But he is our Father and he is persistent. He was patient with Israel as he prepared lovingly to invade the world in the Incarnation, and he is also patient with us. He is determined to bring us into an intimate personal union. He holds us in his arms, waiting for us to recognize him. He wants to spend time with us in what can become the deepest, most intimate union we will ever know.

Thus, our fellowship with God should become the most significant relationship in our life. Like all other loves, it goes two ways. God takes the lead, but as he draws us near, we must do something to communicate with him. And that something is prayer.

Prayer is a big term covering many meanings. Under its roomy umbrella you will find such diverse approaches to God as saying formal prayers, conversation, listening, meditation, contemplation, praying Scripture, spiritual reading, singing, silence and much more. Sometimes we might prefer the structured repetition of the

---

OPEN YOUR HEART TO GOD

Many of us learned early in life to define prayer as a lifting of the mind and heart to God. This was an easy definition to memorize—clear and brief. It was a good definition. It taught us that (1) God is far beyond our ordinary experience; (2) prayer entails effort on our part; and (3) prayer involves both our mind and our heart—our understanding and our feelings and our will.

However, the idea of prayer as a raising of our minds and hearts to God seems to me to overstress our own effort and activity in prayer. I suggest that a better approach would be to define prayer as an *opening* of the mind and heart to God. This seems better because the idea of opening stresses receptivity, responsiveness to another. To open to another is to act, but it is to act in such a way that the other remains the dominant partner.

The good pray-er is above all a good listener. Prayer is dialogue; it is a personal encounter in love. When we communicate with someone we care about, we speak and we listen. But even our speaking is responsive: What we say depends upon what the other person has said to us. Otherwise we don't have

rosary. At other moments, spontaneously telling God how we feel. Or just quietly sitting in his presence, saying nothing. But whatever we do when we pray, common to all prayer is a loving experience of God. It is our personal reply to his gentle intrusion into our life.

Once God gets your attention you can no longer take a casual approach to prayer. Saying an occasional "Our Father" or "Hail

real dialogue, but rather two monologues running along side by side.

Prayer is essentially a dialogic encounter between God and us; and since God is Lord, he alone can initiate the encounter. Hence what we do or say in prayer will depend on what God does or says first.

At the same time, what we do or say is an integral part of prayer, since even God cannot speak *with* us unless we also speak. Prayer does entail effort on our part even though it is always God who reaches across infinity to us, and even though our effort is itself impossible without the sustaining grace of God.

Moreover, our response involves both our head and our heart since we cannot love what we do not know. As Teresa of Avila says, "The important thing [in prayer] is not to think much but to love much." The goal of our prayer is the encounter with God in love. And love, as Teresa goes on to say, "consists, not in the extent of our happiness, but in the firmness of our determination to try to please God in everything."

Adapted from Thomas H. Green, S.J., *Opening to God: A Personal Guide to Prayer for Today* (Ave Maria: 800-282-1865), 20, 24, 25–26.

Mary" is not enough to hold up your part of your relationship with him. Giving ourselves to God in response to his giving himself to us requires regular prayer. We expect to invest a lot of time and energy to maintain our human relationships, as I plan to do, for example, with Alex. But you must expect to invest even more heavily in your divine relationship, which is more important than any of your loves or friendships.

In fact, developing your relationship with God takes daily prayer. That's the only way you're going to be able to foster intimacy with him. If you are not already accustomed to praying every day, it may be difficult for you to find the time. But make time you must because personal union with God is the whole point of Christian living. My recommendation is that you spend prime time with the Lord. You should identify the period of the day when you are most alert and locate your prayer time there. I pray first thing in the morning, which is when I am at my best. Others are at their prime late in the evening long after I have sluggishly shut down my systems. What is your prime time? If you are serious about responding to God, you will reserve some of it every day for personal prayer.

Starting a daily prayer time (or starting over) may require some decisions and arrangements. First, you need to identify a place where you can pray comfortably and without interruption. The "comfortable" may be easy, but for many the "without interruption" may seem impossible. If you are a parent with little children, for example, all life is interruption. You will need to be creative. When the Ghezzi brood of seven was young, my wife and I used to take turns praying, one covering for the other. Maybe that would also work for you.

Second, you will also have to decide what and how you will pray. Prayer is very personal, and no two people pray exactly the same. So I cannot prescribe a formula, but I can describe some principles that will help you grow in prayer.

At the beginning of your prayer time, come into God's presence. Do something to make yourself aware that he is with you. Some people sing a favorite hymn chorus. Others attune themselves to the Lord's presence by reciting traditional prayers or reading aloud from a prayer book. Personally, I mix it up. Some mornings I reflect briefly on each petition of the Lord's Prayer. Other days I pray a favorite psalm or verse that draws me to God, such as: "O God come to my assistance, O Lord make haste to help me." Or sometimes I slowly repeat the Jesus Prayer: "Lord Jesus Christ, Son of the living God, have mercy on me, a sinner." Experiment until you find a way that works for you.

Ask the Holy Spirit to help you pray. Few people feel that they know how to pray the way they ought to. I know I don't. We need a helper and we have one in the Holy Spirit. Inspiring us to love the Father and the Son is part of his work. So wise pray-ers always invoke his assistance. Some simply invite the Spirit to lead them, using their own words. Others pray the traditional "Come, Holy Spirit" (see box on p. 74) or the "Hymn to the Holy Spirit," the beautiful prayer from the Pentecost liturgy (see box p. 98). Once we invoke his aid, we should just go ahead and pray, expecting that he is prompting our thoughts and desires.

Experiment with different forms and modes of prayer to enrich your experience. Try repetitive prayers like the rosary or the Jesus Prayer. Dip into a prayer book where you will find classic and contemporary prayers. Pray the psalms, the Bible's songs of praise. Read Scripture and prayerfully reflect on the verses. Spend

---

COME, HOLY SPIRIT

Come, Holy Spirit, fill the hearts of your faithful,
and enkindle in them the fire of your love.

Send forth your Spirit and they shall be created; and you
shall renew the face of the earth.

Let us pray. O God, who by the light of the Holy Spirit
has instructed the hearts of the faithful, grant by the same
Spirit we may be truly wise and ever rejoice in his consola-
tion through Christ our Lord. Amen.

---

quiet time just listening to God in your heart. Vary your modes of
prayer. For example, we are taught that all prayer falls into one of
four categories summed up in the acronym ACTS: Adoration.
Confession. Thanksgiving. Supplication. I think most of us find
repenting, thanking and asking easier than adoring, so be sure to
make time just to praise the Lord.

Even though God takes the initiative, we should expect to
work hard at praying. That's especially true when we are getting
started. Many a day we will have to force ourselves because we
will not feel like praying. But pray we must. St. Teresa of Avila,
one of the Church's greatest teachers on the subject, compares
our part in praying to the work of irrigating a garden. At first, she
says, praying requires a great deal of effort, as if we were carrying
buckets or pumping water from a well. As we get more experienced at it, she says, our prayer may flow like a stream or even
drench us like a rainstorm. But before the rain comes, we must
persist at our praying.[1]

When we feel as though we have prayed poorly, we can get discouraged. We may even get depressed over it and be tempted to quit. I used to feel that way, but then I learned to stop evaluating my prayer because I am my own worst judge. You are also probably extra hard on yourself. Let God judge the quality of your prayer. You may give yourself a low grade for a prayer time marked with boredom and distraction. But for the same prayer God may award you the highest grade because you fought through and put him first in your thoughts.

Well, what do you say we get started? No time like the present to turn to God. Oops! Alex just banged me on the knee with a cell phone. What do you think? Maybe I am getting through to him.

FOR REFLECTION AND DISCUSSION

1. What does "entering God's presence" mean to me?

2. In what ways does God seem to have invaded my life? How have I responded to him?

3. Why is casual prayer not enough? Do I pray regularly? What can I do differently to ensure that I pray more?

4. What things might I do to improve the way I pray?

5. How does my prayer affect the way I live?

ACTION IDEAS

For those who want to start or restart regular daily prayer:

• Identify both a twenty-minute block of time and a place where you can be alone with God. Make a commitment to this prayer time for one month. Then evaluate your effort, make any necessary adjustments and renew your decision.

For those who want to enhance their daily prayer:

- Build periods of listening into your prayer time. Pause, for example, after praying formal prayers or reading Scripture to allow the Lord to speak in your thoughts. Ask yourself, What is God saying to me today? How can I best respond to him?

- At the beginning of each prayer time, invite the Holy Spirit to lead you. Let him enlarge your experience by increasing your knowledge of God and filling your heart with love.

R E A D   M E !

- *Catechism of the Catholic Church*, Part IV.

- *The Catholic Prayer Book* (Servant Publications: 734-677-6490) is a good collection of classic and contemporary prayers.

- Thomas Green, S.J., *Opening to God: A Personal Guide to Prayer for Today* (Ave Maria: 800-282-1865) is an excellent book for people who want to learn to pray.

- *New Covenant* (Our Sunday Visitor: 800-348-2440) is a magazine devoted to Catholic spirituality.

The Bible as Soul Food

U nless you're a teenager who eats constantly, sporadically or unpredictably, you eat three regular meals daily. You do it because your body demands it and your health depends upon it. You wouldn't think of feasting once a month and not eating the rest of the time. It just wouldn't work.

You may not have thought of it this way, but reading Scripture is to our soul as eating is to our body. The Bible is true "soul food." Jesus himself made this point when the devil tempted him to turn stones into bread: "It is written," he said, "'Man shall not live by bread alone, but by every word that proceeds from the mouth of God'" (Mt 4:4). Thus, reading Scripture is a main source of our spiritual nutrition. If we only read it occasionally, our spirit will be undernourished. If we don't read it at all, our soul may starve. Our spiritual health, therefore, demands that we read the Bible—every day.

Let me say a few more things to persuade you of the importance of regularly reading Scripture. The Bible is the written Word of God himself. It communicates his unfathomable love for human beings and his death-defying plan to give us eternal life. The forty-six books of the Old Testament tell of God's patient work with his people, Israel, which laid the foundation for the accomplishment of his grand design. The New Testament's twenty-seven books convey the denouement of the story of God's love for us: how his Son, Jesus, through his death, resurrection and the sending of the Holy Spirit fulfilled his plan by establishing the New Israel—the Church.

The Bible is unlike any other book. When you read other books, you don't encounter the person who wrote it. So far as you're concerned the author may as well be dead because you will never meet him in the pages of his book. But Scripture is the living Word of God. The Author who inspired the Bible dwells there. The Church recognizes the presence of the Lord in Scripture by the reverence it shows the gospel book during Mass. Our awe before the presence of God in that book is second only to our adoration of the Real Presence in the consecrated host.

When you read the Bible, you not only can discover the will of God in general; you can let him tell you personally what he wants of you. Jesus himself, who patterned his human life on Scripture, taught about this. Once when his disciples urged him to eat something, he declined, saying, "My food is to do the will of him who sent me, and to accomplish his work" (Jn 4:34). Jesus meant for us to do the same. So, can you think of a good reason why we should not be "devouring" the Bible? I can't.

Starting regular Bible study requires us to make several practical decisions:

- Make a commitment to read the Bible for a specified time every day. In *Reading Scripture as the Word of God*, George Martin recommends we set aside fifteen minutes a day. Experience has taught him that fifteen minutes is "just right"—long enough to read intelligently and spiritually, and not so long as to become burdensome.

- Select a Bible that you like to read. Like many Catholics, I choose to read the New American Bible, which is the translation we hear proclaimed during Mass. I also use the Catholic edition of the Revised Standard Version. Numerous other translations are available. It's wise, however, to be sure you are using a Catholic edition of the Bible you prefer.

GOD SPEAKS TO US IN SCRIPTURE

God will speak to those who prayerfully read the Bible as his word. He will not speak in an audible voice; he will not even form words in our mind. His speaking will use no other words than the words that we read—but those words will take on meaning and become alive as if God were present speaking them directly to us. We will have a strong sense that the words of Scripture are indeed addressed to us and are talking about us. We will have a sense that they have a meaning and application in our own lives and specific situations. The Bible will not be merely God's word, but God's word to me. Our hearts will burn within us as we read—not with violent emotion but with the gentle touch of the Holy Spirit, a peaceful presence within us, an assurance that the Father indeed loves us and calls us by name.

George Martin, *Reading Scripture as the Word of God* (Servant Publications: 734-677-6490), 59.

- Schedule a time and place for daily reading. Otherwise you will not stick to your resolve to do it. Currently, for example, first thing in the morning before anyone else is up, I slip into my favorite chair in the living room to read John. What's the best time and place for you?

- Decide where to start. You should avoid the common mistake of beginning at Genesis and reading through to Revelation. I tried that once and got as far as Leviticus before I gave up. That's an unwise approach not only because it's tedious but also because the Bible was not designed to be read that way. The Bible is a library of books in one volume. While there is a rationale to the placement of books, they are not arranged in a chronological order. Some books of the Old Testament, for example, should be read in the perspective of books in the New Testament. If you are plunging in for the first time, you might start with the Gospel of Luke and the Acts of the Apostles or the Gospel of Mark. Then turn to Paul's letters to the Thessalonians and the Corinthians.

Reading Scripture is as much a matter of the heart as it is of the head. Consequently, we should prepare ourselves with prayer. Sometimes, for example, I pray the traditional "Come, Holy Spirit" (see box on p. 74). I figure since the Spirit inspired the original words, he can open their meaning for me now. And often as not, reading a passage leads to praying with it, an activity in which the Holy Spirit is supremely interested. Here's another prayer you might find useful.

PRAYER BEFORE READING SCRIPTURE

Lord, your Word is a lamp for my feet, guiding me to truth and wisdom. Send the Holy Spirit to help me understand it and apply it faithfully so that I might enjoy eternal life, through Jesus Christ, my Savior. Amen.

Intelligent Bible reading requires that we ask the right questions of the text. The Church teaches us that the primary meaning of Scripture is what the human writer intended to convey to his readers when writing under the inspiration of the Holy Spirit (see box). To get at the heart of a passage, therefore, we must ask this question: What point was the author trying to make to his audience? A second question will help us discover what the Holy Spirit is saying to us through the passage: What does this text mean for me today?

HOW CATHOLICS INTERPRET SCRIPTURE

Those divinely revealed realities which are contained and presented in Sacred Scripture have been committed to writing under the inspiration of the Holy Spirit.... In composing the sacred books, God chose men and while employed by Him they made use of their powers and abilities, so that with Him acting in them and through them, they, as true authors, consigned to writing everything and only those things which He wanted.

Therefore, since everything asserted by the inspired authors or sacred writers must be held to be asserted by the Holy Spirit, it follows that the books of Scripture must be acknowledged as teaching firmly, faithfully, and without error that truth which God wanted put into the sacred writings for the sake of our salvation....

However, since God speaks in Sacred Scripture through men in human fashion, the interpreter of Sacred Scripture, in order to see clearly what God wanted to communicate to us, should carefully investigate what meaning the sacred writers really intended, and what God wanted to manifest by means of their words.

Vatican Council II, *Dogmatic Constitution on Divine Revelation [Dei Verbum],* 11–12

Using these questions enables us to dig until we get to the kernel of God's Word.

Now and then we depart from our usual menu and treat ourselves to a banquet or to dinner out at a nice restaurant. There is a parallel here for our Bible reading. Occasionally we should set aside more time and do some serious Scripture study. We might, for example, read the Gospel of Mark at one or two sittings. Then, with the help of a commentary or other study aid, work our way through it again systematically. I have studied different books of the Bible like that once a year for the past decade. Each time the experience has been unforgettable, and the lessons I have learned have been life-changing. I recommend that you consider such a feast yourself. Eat hearty.

FOR REFLECTION AND DISCUSSION

1. Why is reading Scripture essential for my Christian life?

2. What makes the Bible different from all other books?

3. How often do I read the Bible? What would I need to do to read it more regularly?

4. Why is it important to figure out what the writer of Scripture really intended? How can we find out what Scripture is saying to us today?

ACTION IDEAS

1. Promise yourself that for the next month you will spend fifteen minutes a day, at least five days a week, reading one of the Gospels. Each day ask what the writer intended to say and what

the text is saying to you now. At the end of the month, reflect on your experience. Then do it again.

2. Enhance your prayer time by praying one of the psalms each day until you have worked your way through the entire book. Notice which psalms draw you nearer to God so that you can return to them later on.

3. Invite a few family members or friends to join with you in a weekly Bible study for a three-month period. Set aside one hour at a mutually agreed upon time, and agree to stop when the hour is up. Select a book of the New Testament to begin with, perhaps the Gospel of Luke or Mark. Consider using a good Catholic study guide. At the beginning of the hour, read aloud the text for the evening. Then everyone can share what they think the writer was saying and what the text says to them.

R E A D   M E !

- Vatican Council II, *Dogmatic Constitution on Divine Revelation [Dei Verbum]* (Pauline Books & Media: 800-876-4463) is the main source for Catholic teaching on the Bible.

- George Martin, *Reading Scripture as the Word of God* (Servant Publications: 734-677-6490) is the best popular introduction to Bible reading and study for Catholics.

- *God's Word Today* is a daily Scripture reading and study guide for Catholics published by *Catholic Digest* (800-335-7771).

- The Liturgical Press (800-858-5450) publishes *The Collegeville Bible Commentary.* It is an excellent series of inexpensive, popular Catholic commentaries on the books of the Bible.

NINE

Mary, the Saints and You

L ast year hundreds of thousands of pilgrims made their way to an office center in Clearwater, Florida. They came daily by the carloads to view a nine-story image of a woman's veiled head clearly etched in the building's glass exterior. Many believed that the huge picture was an apparition of the Virgin Mary. The authenticity of such a phenomenon is for the Church to judge. But in my view the piety of many of the pilgrims was genuine. They came to pray, to seek God's help, to repent. Devotion to Mary seemed to have brought them closer to her Son.

Popular devotion to Mary is no novelty. Catholics have venerated her for many centuries. By agreeing to become the mother of Jesus, Mary received a unique role in God's plan, a special collaboration in bringing salvation to humanity (see box on p. 86). We have also honored as saints other women and men who have lived ordinary Christian lives in extraordinary ways. Observing the excesses of some Catholics, critics have often falsely accused the Church of putting these fellow human beings in God's place and adoring them. Catholics, however, do not worship Mary or the saints. We revere them, esteem them, celebrate them and hold them up as examples—yes. But *adore* them? Never, since worship and adoration belong to God alone.

Through a rigorous process called canonization, the Church scrutinizes the lives of holy women and men to ensure that they have lived faithful Christian lives and are now united with God in heaven. Because they have already received their heavenly reward,

MOTHER MARY

There is but one mediator, as we know from the words of the Apostle: "For there is one God, and one mediator between God and men, the man Christ Jesus, who gave himself as a ransom for all." The maternal duty of Mary toward men in no way obscures or diminishes this unique mediation of Christ, but rather shows His power. For all the salvific influence of the Blessed Virgin on men originates, not from some inner necessity, but from the divine pleasure. It flows forth from the superabundance of the merits of Christ, rests on His mediation, depends entirely on it, and draws all its power from it. In no way does it impede, but rather does it foster the immediate union of the faithful with Christ.

Predestined from eternity by that decree of divine providence which determined the incarnation of the Word to be the Mother of God, the Blessed Virgin was on this earth the virgin Mother of the Redeemer, and above all others and in a singular way the generous associate and humble handmaid of the Lord. She conceived, brought forth, and nourished Christ. She presented Him to the Father in the temple, and was united with Him by compassion as He died on the Cross. In this singular way she cooperated by her obedience, faith, hope and burning charity in the work of the Savior in giving back supernatural life to souls. Wherefore she is our mother in the order of grace.

This maternity of Mary in the order of grace began with the consent which she gave in faith at the Annunciation and which she sustained without wavering beneath the cross, and lasts until the eternal fulfillment of all the elect. Taken up to heaven, she did not lay aside this salvific duty, but by her constant intercession continued to bring us the gifts of eternal salvation.

Vatican Council II, *The Dogmatic Constitution on the Church [Lumen Gentium]*, 60–62.

the saints are sometimes collectively described as "The Church Triumphant." In Christ they are still connected to us in what the Apostles' Creed calls "the communion of saints." Thus, Mary and the saints are our forebears in the Body of Christ.

Since the saints are in heaven and have direct, face-to-face access to God, we ask them to intercede with the Lord for our needs and intentions. How does this differ from worship? Praying to Mary and the saints is like inviting your earthly mother, relatives and friends to join you in asking God for something. Except we can expect better results because Mary and the saints can pray more effectively than our earthly intercessors due to their closeness to God in heaven. "Don't weep, for I shall be more useful to you after my death," said St. Dominic to his colleagues, "and I shall help you then more effectively than during my life." What could he have meant, except that once in heaven he would take their concerns directly to the Lord? And St. Thérèse of Lisieux died in obscurity, but after her death became the most popular of modern saints because thousands of miracles have occurred through her intercession.

The word *saint* derives from a Latin root that means "holy" or "consecrated." In that sense, we are all saints because the Holy Spirit is in us and lets us share his holiness. His presence makes it possible for us to become more Christlike because he alone enables our feeble wills to obey Jesus' seemingly outrageous and impossible commands: "Love one another as I have loved you" (Jn 15:12). Or: "Love your enemies and pray for those who persecute you" (Mt 5:44). And try this one: "You, therefore, must be perfect, as your heavenly Father is perfect" (Mt 5:48). The Spirit helped Mary and the saints navigate their lives according to Jesus' directives. He's there to strengthen us to rise to the same challenge.

Thus, Mary and the saints are our mentors in Christian living. They show us how to behave as daughters and sons of God. We are no longer mere human beings, but members of God's family, living supernatural lives. But we quickly forget who we really are. So we watch the saints to see how it's done—how ordinary humans can live divinized lives. They imitated Christ and became like him; so by following their example we can hope to become Christlike, too.

For example, consider what we learn from Mary. Her simple "yes" at the Annunciation demonstrated for us that submission and obedience are our appropriate responses to God's initiatives in our life. At the Cana wedding Mary taught us how to approach Jesus boldly with expectant faith. Standing beneath the cross, she was the exemplar of perseverance amid unimaginable suffering. We can expand this short list by reflecting on her behavior at her other life experiences: her visit to Elizabeth, the birth of Christ, the prophecies at Jesus' circumcision, the flight to Egypt, finding the lost child Jesus in the Temple, Jesus' public ministry, receiving the Holy Spirit in the Upper Room at Pentecost, and so on.

Every saint is an "original" and also has unique lessons for us. I have been reading of saints' lives again over the past two years, and here are some things that they are teaching me:

- Twice St. Anthony of Egypt made significant changes in his life in response to a Gospel he heard proclaimed at Mass. Even though sometimes I think I'm allergic to change, his example makes me listen more carefully during the Liturgy of the Word.

- St. Catherine of Siena was simultaneously a woman of deep prayer and a vigorous social activist—a model of true spirituality. Watching her prompts me to pray with more fervor and look for more ways to care for others.

- St. Thérèse of Lisieux aspired to the heights of Christian service. She wanted to be a martyr, but settled for simply doing whatever love required. She calls me to the daily practical martyrdom of saying no to myself so I can say yes to someone else.

- My wife and kids will testify that I am a poor listener. So I am striving to pay more attention to others, imitating the compassion of Venerable Solanus Casey. For forty years he spent twelve hours a day listening to people's troubles and counseling them.

- St. Therese Margaret of the Sacred Heart was sickly, but was so full of thankfulness to God for everything, that she brought cheer to everyone around her. I have a strong preference to be grumpy when things go wrong, but with this lovely saint in mind, I'm working at thanking God in all circumstances.

Overall, observing Mary and the saints has taught me two profound, topsy-turvy truths at the heart of Christianity. First, it's not we who are on a search for God, but God himself who comes after us, as he did the lovely Jewish teenager he chose to become the Mother of his Son. Second, we don't have to figure out God's "plan for our life" and struggle to accomplish it. All we need to do

---

THE MEMORARE

Remember, O most gracious Virgin Mary, that never was it known that anyone who fled to your protection, implored your help or sought your intercession was left unaided. Inspired by this confidence, I fly to you, O Virgin of Virgins, my Mother. To you I come, before you I stand sinful and sorrowful. O Mother of the Word Incarnate, despise not my petitions, but in your mercy hear and answer me. Amen.

is surrender to him and let his desires guide us from day to day, just like Mary and the saints did. For me these are very freeing and consoling realities.

"You can observe a lot just by watching," said Yogi Berra. And when we watch the saints closely, we observe something other than their goodness. We notice their flaws sticking out from among their virtues. The saints frequently declared themselves to be the worst sinners. Perhaps some were before they gave their lives to Christ. Paul, Mary Magdalene and Augustine, to name a few. Saints struggled daily with difficulties: Margaret of Cortona with guilt feelings, Jerome with anger and lust, Thérèse of Lisieux with scruples. Seeing the saints' weaknesses encourages us, not that we rejoice in their wrongs. But knowing the saints were just like us—human beings subject to sin, worry, failure, grief, temptation and the like—gives us some hope. If these women and men can make it, I say to myself, maybe with a little help so can I. OK, OK, alot of help.

FOR REFLECTION AND DISCUSSION

1. Why do we honor Mary and the saints? What role do they play in our lives?

2. How does the honor we give Mary and the saints differ from the worship we give to God?

3. In what sense can we say that Mary is our mother?

4. How is it possible for a person to become a saint?

5. What kinds of lessons can we learn by observing the saints?

ACTION IDEAS

1. For the next month, make intercession to Mary or to a particular saint a part of your daily prayer. Select a concern, big or little, and ask Mary or the saint to join you in praying about it. Use your own words or choose a formal prayer such as the Memorare (see box on p. 89). Consider making this a regular practice.

2. Reflect on the life of Mary presented in these Scriptures: Matthew 1:18-25; Matthew 2:1-23; Luke 1:26-56; Luke 2; John 2:1-12; John 19:25-27. Meditate on one chapter each day for a week, or take it more slowly, spreading your reading over a longer period. Be sure to ask these questions: What was the Gospel writer trying to say? and What does this text say to me? Your goal in this activity should be to identify one thing you could do to imitate Mary in your life.

3. Select two or three saints and read about them. Look for answers to questions like: How did this saint come to know God? How did he or she respond to God? In what ways did the saint apply the gospel to his or her life? What were this saint's weaknesses? How did he or she deal with them? What is the main lesson I can take away from observing this saint? Look for one thing that you can do to imitate these saints.

R E A D   M E !

- Bert Ghezzi, *Miracles of the Saints: True Stories of Lives Touched by the Supernatural* (Zondervan: 800-727-3480).

- LaVonne Neff, *Breakfast With the Saints* (Servant Publications: 734-677-6490) has an excellent appendix guiding readers to books about the saints.

- Edward D. O'Connor, C.S.C., *The Catholic Vision* (Our Sunday Visitor: 800-348-2440), 446–60, is a compact exposition of Catholic teaching on Mary.

TEN

Meet the Holy Spirit, the Worker

The New Testament uses several vibrant symbols to represent the Holy Spirit. These images are instructive because they depict the Spirit's relation to us. At his baptism Jesus saw the Spirit descending and settling on him as a dove (see Mt 3:16). Jesus himself declared that believers would have the Holy Spirit flowing from within like rivers of living water (see Jn 7:37). After Jesus' resurrection when the disciples huddled expectantly in the Upper Room, the Spirit came upon them as tongues of fire (see Acts 2:3). So the Holy Spirit comes to us vigorously. He is active and energetic. Lively as a dove. Dynamic as a river. Fiery.

Personally, I sometimes imagine the Holy Spirit appearing as a worker bearing a toolbox. I know this is not a biblical representation, and I have never seen anything like it in Christian art. No icon, sculpture or painting of *The Holy Spirit, the Worker*. Perhaps I got the idea because I think of the Spirit as my Helper, which is a very loose paraphrase of Paraclete, one of his names in Scripture (see Jn 14:16).

Because he is dynamic, active and energetic, my picture of the Holy Spirit, the Worker is, appropriately, a movie. In the opening scene, the bishop is extending his hands and praying for the Holy Spirit to come upon us. He lays hands on us, anointing us with blessed oil. Immediately in the next frame, the Holy Spirit, the Worker briskly enters our lives afresh. He opens his box and presents each of us with seven tools or workings as his gifts: wisdom, understanding, knowledge, counsel, fortitude, fear of the Lord and piety. Then he plants nine seeds that will grow into the fruit of the Spirit (see chapter twelve). And we get to write, produce and direct the rest of the movie. The story and its outcome depend on how we use the tools and grow the fruit that the Spirit gives us.

My dad was a carpenter, and somewhere packed away in the attic I have a collection of his tools. I remember that I didn't know the purpose of a few of his unusual gadgets. Of course, I recognized some of Dad's tools—an awl, drill bits and chisels—but I never used any of them. Sometimes I have treated the Holy Spirit's tools in the same way. I have packed them up and forgotten about them. But lately I have become determined to receive the benefits of these valuable gifts.

The seven spiritual gifts are not ornaments for display on the mantels of our souls. Nor does the Spirit actually give them to us

---

CONFIRMATION CONFERS THE SPIRIT AND HIS GIFTS

All-powerful God, the Father of our Lord Jesus Christ,
by water and the Holy Spirit
you freed your sons and daughters from sin
and gave them new life.
Send your Holy Spirit upon them
to be their helper and guide.
Give them the spirit of wisdom and understanding,
the spirit of right judgment and courage,
the spirit of knowledge and reverence.
Fill them with the spirit of wonder and awe in your presence.
We ask this through Christ our Lord.

Prayer from the Rite of Confirmation

as our possessions. Rather, they are gifts that he exercises in us. They are his divine workings that strengthen us for daily Christian living. The Holy Spirit, the Worker, employs these gifts in us so that we may build lives that serve God, the Church and all humanity. Thus, they are very practical resources.

Isaiah the prophet first cataloged these gifts as workings of the Spirit who would rest on the Messiah (see Is 11:2). Now they are spiritual gifts operative in all of us who are members of Christ. Four of them enlighten our minds:

Wisdom is divine guidance that helps us to know and conform to God's ways. I think it was wisdom, for example, that led me to reduce my heavy requirements on a teenage son, when my own idea was to hold his feet to the fire. The Spirit was nudging me to be merciful as God is, and as a result of my obedience, my son is nearer to God than my strictness could have taken him.

With *understanding* the Holy Spirit deepens our insight into Christian mysteries. My whole outlook changed, for example, when the Spirit caused me to see that Christ counts on me as a member of his body to serve others in his name.

Counsel is Holy Spirit-inspired prudence which equips us to discern and to avoid spiritual obstacles. He is *counseling* me when I know deep down that if I say one more sentence in a heated conversation, I will lose control of my temper. If I am listening to the Spirit, I will shut up and walk away.

The Spirit uses *knowledge* to open us to God and to reveal his will for our lives. Once, for instance, a teacher asked me if I had any experience of God when I prayed. I suspect it was the Holy Spirit letting me *know* that the Father wanted me to pray more seriously and with more fervor. So I did, and guess what!—I got to know him a little better.

The three remaining spiritual gifts strengthen our wills:

Fortitude is a working of the Spirit that empowers us to obey the Lord even in difficult circumstances. It is the courage that the Holy Spirit gives martyrs to prepare them to endure torture and death. On a smaller scale, fortitude is the grace I receive to hold myself and my family to high moral standards in a society that seems to have lost its moorings.

The Spirit fills us with *fear of the Lord* to convince us to submit to God's authority. St. Catherine of Siena, for example, often saw condemned criminals repent when she prayed that the Spirit would make them fear God. And as I get older and death seems less like a remote possibility, I think that fear of the Lord is working more in me to my great benefit.

Last, though not least, is *piety,* the divinely inspired awe that sets our hearts aflame with devotion to God. It sums up our responses to the divine presence in our lives. Piety is the motivation for our prayer, study and service and the driver of our love for God and for others.

These spiritual gifts have been operative in many of us since our youth, but often at a much lower level than is possible. Perhaps like me you've packaged them up and let them lie dormant.

You can engage the Spirit and activate his gifts simply by praying. Ask him in your own words to come to you afresh, or use one of the great ancient prayers (see box on page 98). Then expect him to act because he's right there waiting to plunge in and do something for you. So, if you'd like to experience a little dynamism in your Christian life—maybe some living water or some fire—you can meet the Holy Spirit, the Worker and surrender to him.

THE FRIEND CLOSEST
TO OUR HEARTS

Jesus taught us to relate to the Father as "Abba." The apostles and disciples learned to relate to Jesus with warmth and friendship. How shall we imagine the person of the Holy Spirit in order to relate to the Spirit with the same depth of love and intimacy?

In John's Gospel, Jesus indicates that in some ways the Holy Spirit would be even closer to the apostles than he was—as teacher, counselor and witness within their hearts. He would be the "paraclete," one who is called to be at a person's side, a companion, a friend. Based on this, I would like to suggest a personal image of the Holy Spirit that embodies all that he is and does for us: the Holy Spirit is "the friend closest to our hearts."

Granted, this is not a biblical image, but it is found in the early Christian writers, the Fathers of the Church. For example, St. Cyril of Jerusalem taught, "The Spirit comes with the tenderness of a true friend and protector to save, to heal, to teach, to counsel, to strengthen, to console." Most of all this image reminds us that the Holy Spirit is someone with whom we can speak and relate in an intimate, personal way. He is truly the divine friend who is closest to our hearts.

Adapted from Alan Schreck, *Hearts Aflame: The Holy Spirit at the Heart of Christian Life Today* (Servant Publications: 734-677-6490), 25–26.

HYMN TO THE HOLY SPIRIT

Holy Spirit, font of light,
　　focus of God's glory bright,
　　shed on us a shining ray.
Father of the fatherless,
　　giver of gifts limitless,
　　come and touch our hearts today.
Source of strength and sure relief,
　　comforter in time of grief,
　　enter in and be our guest.
On our journey grant us aid,
　　freshening breeze and cooling shade,
　　in our labor inward rest.
Enter each aspiring heart,
　　occupy its inmost part
　　with your dazzling purity.
All that gives to man his worth,
　　all that benefits the earth,
　　you bring to maturity.
With your soft refreshing rains
　　break our drought, remove our stains;
　　bind up all our injuries.
Shake with rushing wind our will;
　　melt with fire our icy chill;
　　bring to light our perjuries.
As your promise we believe
　　make us ready to receive
　　gifts from your unbounded store.
Grant enabling energy,
　　courage in adversity,
　　joys that last for evermore.[1]

FOR REFLECTION AND DISCUSSION

1. In what ways is the Holy Spirit our Helper and our Friend? Why might he be called the Worker?

2. How have I experienced the work of the Holy Spirit in my life?

3. What are the gifts of the Holy Spirit we receive in confirmation?

4. Which of these gifts am I in most need of now? Is there anything I can do to engage this gift more completely in my life?

5. Do I expect the Holy Spirit to work in my life? What can I do to relate to him more personally?

ACTION IDEAS

1. If you feel that the action of the Holy Spirit in your experience has been somewhat impersonal, muted or "on hold," pray and ask the Lord to release him in your life. Expect him to act, for he will work in every part of your being.

2. Refresh your life in the Holy Spirit by praying daily the "Hymn to the Holy Spirit" (see box on p. 98). Pay close attention to the words and phrases and look for results, for you can count on the Spirit to hear your prayer.

3. If you are baptized, but not confirmed, make arrangements with your parish to receive the sacrament of confirmation. The parish will want you to prepare yourself by attending some classes that will ensure your readiness for this important step.

R E A D   M E !

- The *Catechism of the Catholic Church* (#683–747) sums up Catholic teaching on the Holy Spirit.

- Edward D. O'Connor, C.S.C., *The Catholic Vision* (Our Sunday Visitor: 800-348-2440), Part 5, 330–62.

- Alan Schreck, *Hearts Aflame: The Holy Spirit at the Heart of Christian Life Today* (Servant Publications: 734-677-6490) is a popular explanation of the Holy Spirit and his work.

Making Daily Changes

"God's laws help us to tell right from wrong. But knowing what's right is one thing, and doing it is another. We may solemnly announce to God and ourselves, for example, that from now on we are going to obey a certain command, only to discover that our will is not strong enough to enforce our decision.

"Well aware of our human weaknesses, God has provided us help for obeying his laws. A Helper, in fact. For he sent the Holy Spirit to enable us to conform to his ways."

ELEVEN

Doing the Right Thing

Put on your thinking cap and see if you can remember all of the Ten Commandments. Don't worry about getting them in the right order. Just list as many of the Ten Commandments as you can. Go ahead, write them in the spaces below.

_____

_____

_____

_____

_____

_____

_____

_____

_____

_____

Well, how did you do? Congratulations if you got them all. If you missed any, you'd better look up the ones you couldn't remember (see box on p. 104). You may need to do something about them. For unlike Frank, a comic-strip character who told his buddy Ernest he was going to practice doing the Ten

Commandments one at a time, we can't be choosy. Our happiness depends on our obeying them all simultaneously.

The Bible calls the Ten Commandments "the Decalogue," that is, the "ten words" of God. As such they are the *first* word—not the *last* word—of Catholic morality. They are, however, the place to start since God revealed them as his foundational laws for his people. The first three commandments indicate our obligations to God. The last seven spell out our responsibilities to our neighbors.

THE TEN COMMANDMENTS

This traditional version of the Ten Commandments is based on Exodus 20:2-17 and Deuteronomy 5:6-21:

I.   I am the Lord your God:
you shall not have strange Gods before me.

II.   You shall not take the name of the Lord
your God in vain.

III.   Remember to keep holy the Lord's Day.

IV.   Honor your father and your mother.

V.   You shall not kill.

VI.   You shall not commit adultery.

VII.   You shall not steal.

VIII.   You shall not bear false witness against
your neighbor.

IX.   You shall not covet your neighbor's wife.

X.   You shall not covet your neighbor's goods.

God wove the commandments into the fabric of his creation. Because he put these laws in the nature of things, God himself couldn't change one of them even if he started again from scratch. However, the Ten Commandments are not the arbitrary "thou shalt nots" of a divine dictator. They are laws that a loving Father has given us to ensure our spiritual welfare.

The Decalogue is the spinal column of the Christian life, say theologians Susan Muto and Adrian van Kaam. It forms the backbone of our spiritual health. And Dominican theologian Augustine DiNoia describes the commandments as God's rules for spiritual fitness. We all know about the rules for physical fitness, that eating right and exercising regularly will enhance our well-being. "Similarly," says DiNoia, "obeying the Ten Commandments will make us spiritually fit." It comes down to this: If we conform to God's ways which are summed up in these ten laws, we will be happy and spiritually healthy. If we don't obey the Ten Commandments, we will be spiritually unfit and miserable.

Management consultants teach companies the 80/20 rule. It holds that 20 percent of their business activity accounts for accomplishing 80 percent of their goals. Jesus did something like that with the Ten Commandments. When we obey the two great commandments—loving God and loving our neighbor—Jesus said we are obeying all of the Ten Commandments (see Mt 22:40). Thus, Jesus also transformed the "thou shalt nots" into "thou shalts," elevating the prohibitions into positive actions. As Paul said to the Romans, "The commandments, 'You shall not commit adultery, You shall not kill, You shall not steal, You shall not covet,' and any other commandment, are summed up in this sentence, 'You shall love your neighbor as yourself.' Love does no wrong to a neighbor; therefore love is the fulfilling of the law" (Rom 13:9-10).

Love God. Love others. Well, that should be easy enough to

do, shouldn't it? I wish that were true, but it's not so. My intentions are good enough, but honestly I don't always do the things I should to love God above all. Certainly, I don't always do the loving thing to my family, let alone my neighbors. You may be in the same boat. Something in our humanity weighs us down and keeps us from obeying the commandments.

God's laws help us to tell right from wrong. But knowing what's right is one thing, and doing it is another. We may solemnly announce to God and ourselves, for example, that from now on we are going to obey a certain command, only to discover that our will is not strong enough to enforce our decision.

Well aware of our human weaknesses, God has provided us help for obeying his laws. A Helper, in fact. For he sent the Holy Spirit to enable us to conform to his ways. He does that by transforming us in the image of Christ. By making us like Christ, who obeyed his Father in everything.

God's intervention, however, does not relieve us of the responsibility to act. We still must determine to do the loving thing in every situation. But instead of gritting our teeth and compelling ourselves to do what we know is right, we must simply decide to behave as Christ would.

Christian moral behavior, says C.S. Lewis, is a matter of two children's games: "let's play dress up" and "let's pretend."[1] First, we must "dress up" like Christ. "Put on the Lord Jesus Christ," said Paul, "and make no provision for the flesh, to gratify its desires" (Rom 13:14). Every morning we should put on Christ as we would put on a fresh set of clothes. Then as we go about our day we need not worry about doing the right thing. Having put on Christ, we will learn to conduct ourselves in all of our dealings as he would. Note well, however, that "dressing up" like Christ is not hiding our sinfulness behind a costume. Rather, by baptism we

THE REWARD
OF OBEDIENCE

We must appreciate the character-forming power of these ten divine commands. To obey or disobey one of them is to do the same for all. We cannot take one vertebra out of our spinal column and expect to stand up straight. Similarly, we need to live upright lives morally and to develop contemplative traits spiritually. Only then can we come to full maturity in soul, mind, spirit and body. The commandments of God thus offer us the only true approach to holistic or distinctively human formation. Through them, aided by divine grace, each of us can respond uniquely and communally to the universal call of holiness.

What most facilitates these foundational steps to peace and joy is our desire to see God, that is, our desire for true happiness. How reassuring it is to know that to find this treasure we do not need to invent new steps; we need only to turn to the ancient, time-tested truths found in the Ten Commandments....

God not only gives us the way to harmonious unfolding. He himself is the best reward we can attain for following the commandments with strength of character.

Adapted from Susan Muto and Adrian Van Kaam, *The Commandments: Ten Ways to a Happy Life and a Healthy Soul* (Servant Publications: 734-677-6490), 213–15.

have become new creations in Christ (see 2 Cor 5:17). Thus, clothing ourselves with Christ is our appropriate dress.

Secondly, if we want to acquire Christian virtues, Lewis says we must also play "let's pretend." How do we become kind or humble? Surely not just by praying for these qualities. We can pray and pray and still be mean and arrogant. Virtues are actions, so we must do something to develop them. To become kind, we must think of ourself as a kind person and do whatever kindness demands. If we want humility we must pretend to be humble already and put ourselves at the service of others. As we are going through the motions of kindness and humility, Christ is with us making the virtue stick in our character. So if we pretend to be already kind and humble and consistently try to do what kindness and humility require, he will see to it that we acquire these virtues.

Today the Ten Commandments are somewhat out of fashion. Our contemporary culture is not comfortable with absolutes of any kind. Many people agree with Madonna, for example, who recently said she would read the Bible to her daughter, but would also tell the child she did not have to do what it said. They believe that there are no rules, and that what they do is nobody's business but their own.

These views can justify any kind of behavior, so we find them very appealing. Such opinions are also very dangerous because they can help us cozy up to sin. And nonchalance about serious wrongdoing can ultimately have life-threatening consequences for our souls. We would do well to undertake a little self-exam to see if these notions have insinuated themselves into our thinking. I know I find them lurking in my thoughts. Reflecting on the Ten Commandments can help us expose them. They are bright flood lamps that cut through the fog surrounding these popular amoral ideas.

FOR REFLECTION AND DISCUSSION

1. Why can the Ten Commandments be described as God's rules for spiritual fitness?

2. How does obeying the two great love commandments result in our obeying all the commandments?

3. Why do we find it difficult to do the right thing? What help does God give us to obey the commandments?

4. How does "dressing up" like Christ help us to do the right thing?

5. How does "pretending" to have a Christian quality help us to acquire it?

6. What reward can we expect if we pattern our lives on the Ten Commandments?

ACTION IDEAS

1. Study the Ten Commandments as recorded in Exodus 20:2-17 and Deuteronomy 5:6-21. Consider how well your life conforms to the commandments. Ask yourself, What one thing can I do to strengthen my relationship with God? What one thing can I do to improve my relationships with others?

2. Reflect on Romans 13:8-14. Here Paul both explains how obeying the great commandments guarantees obedience to all the others and also exhorts us to "put on Christ." Conduct the following experiment for the next month. First thing each morning affirm two decisions: today I will do the loving thing in every situation, and I am dressing up like Christ so that I can

behave like he would. At the end of the month review your experience.

3. C.S. Lewis says that the way to acquire a virtue is to do the behaviors it requires and expect Christ to work it into our character. Examine your strengths and weaknesses and select one of your lesser weaknesses to work on. (Tackle bigger ones later.) Perhaps you are not as generous or as patient as you would like to be. Make a list of actions that express the virtue you want to acquire. Every day for a month, ask Christ to give you the strength you need to behave differently, and perform one of the actions that dispose you to the virtue you want to acquire.

READ ME!

- The *Catechism of the Catholic Church* (#2052–2557), summarizes Catholic teaching on each of the Ten Commandments.

- C.S. Lewis, *Mere Christianity* (available in many editions). In part three of this book, Lewis reflects practically on Christian moral behavior.

- Susan Muto and Adrian van Kaam, *The Commandments: Ten Ways to a Happy Life and a Healthy Soul* (Servant Publications: 734-677-6490).

TWELVE

Signs of Real Love

I cringe when I see placards proclaiming "John 3:16" popping up at sports events. These may be well-intentioned efforts to announce that God loved us so much he delivered his Son to death to save us. But in my opinion they trivialize the gospel. Those who need to hear the message don't take the verse seriously, and some even make a joke of it. For example, comedians routinely poke fun at it. "I thought someone was trying to get John," said one wag recently, "to come to section 3, row 16."

Sign waving is an inadequate substitute for real evangelization. Instead of using John 3:16 to declare the Good News, we Christians should base our outreach on another text with coincidentally similar numbering—1 John 3:16. And I am not suggesting we write it on signs. We must write it on our lives. It reads: "The way we came to know love was that he laid down his life for us; so we ought to lay down our lives for our brothers" (NAB). If we were truly to imitate Christ's sacrificial love, we would become living signs. People would be intrigued by our behavior because they know in their gut that genuine love is no easy thing. They would wonder what or who made us give up our own selfish desires for others' sake. Jesus himself described the impact our love would have: "This is how all will know that you are my disciples, if you have love for one another" (Jn 13:35, NAB).

Our love, in fact, is the gauge that measures our faith. The Church from the first to the twenty-first centuries and Scripture from Genesis to Revelation have always made love for others the test of our love for God. John, for example, says it most directly: "If any one says, 'I love God,' and hates his brother, he is a liar; for he who does not love his brother whom he has seen, cannot love God whom he has not seen" (1 Jn 4:20).

So if we wonder how we measure up as Christians, we don't have to look very far. All we need to do is to review the condition of our relationships. We can ask ourselves questions like these: How do I treat other Christians? My neighbors? The people at work or at school? How do I relate to my wife? My husband? My children? My parents? Am I kind to others? Do I forgive people? Do I really love others? That's where the rubber hits the road.

None of us finds the demands of love easy. When we try to do the things it requires, we often meet resistance from our own selfish desires. "What she said last night hurt my feelings," we say to ourselves. "Well, it'll be a long time before I forgive her. I may not even talk to her today. Or tomorrow, either." Inclinations like that one regularly clog the flow of love in families and friendships.

We all indulge in behaviors that damage our relationships. Like losing our temper. Or giving the cold shoulder to someone we envy. Or passing on a rumor that hurts someone's reputation. Or hitting on someone with a suggestive remark. Conduct like this is the common heritage of sinful human beings and is rooted in evil tendencies. "When you follow the desires of your sinful nature," says Paul to the Galatians, "your lives will produce these evil results: sexual immorality, impure thoughts, eagerness for lustful pleasure, idolatry, participation in demonic activities, hostility, quarreling, jealousy, outbursts of anger, selfish ambitions, divisions, the feeling that everyone is wrong except those in your own little groups, envy, drunkenness, wild parties and other kinds of sin" (Gal 5:19-21, NLT).

Whew! That's some list. Now, I don't think Paul believed each

WHAT WE MUST DO

Put to death the sinful, earthly things lurking within you. Have nothing to do with sexual sin, impurity, lust and shameful desires. Don't be greedy for the good things of this life, for that is idolatry. God's terrible anger will come upon those who do such things. You used to do them when your life was still part of this world. But now is the time to get rid of anger, rage, malicious behavior, slander, and dirty language. In its place you have clothed yourself with a brand-new nature that is continually being renewed as you learn more and more about Christ, who created this new nature within you....

Since God chose you to be the holy people whom he loves, you must clothe yourselves with tenderhearted mercy, kindness, humility, gentleness, and patience. You must make allowance for each other's faults and forgive the person who offends you. Remember the Lord forgave you, so you must forgive others. And the most important piece of clothing you must wear is love. Love is what binds us all together in perfect harmony. And let the peace that comes from Christ rule in your hearts. For as members of one body you are all called to live in peace. And always be thankful.

Colossians 3:5-15 (NLT)

of us did all these things. But we probably identify with one or two of them. I know I do, and I realize that when I do them they hurt my relationships. For example, my anger diminishes my love. I confess I have had a lifelong battle with it. My long-suffering wife can tell you all about my temper. Mary Lou has never read my little book *The Angry Christian*. "Why do I need to read about the angry Christian?" she says. "I live with him!"

Faced with our negative behavior, we often feel helpless to overcome it. Somehow it seems to recur no matter how hard we work to avoid it. Because our willpower isn't strong enough to resist our habitually bad conduct, we need something beyond ourselves to change it. And that something is a Someone—the Holy Spirit, whom we receive in baptism and confirmation.

When the Holy Spirit comes to us, he brings with him a set of behaviors which are replacements for our evil inclinations and actions. We call these behaviors the fruit of the Spirit—love, joy,

---

BECOMING LIKE CHRIST

The fruit of the Spirit—love, peace, patience, kindness and so on—are not mainly feelings. They are patterns of behavior or character traits. Feelings are internal reactions, but the fruit of the Spirit are chiefly active and external. You can see this in the context of Colossians 3 and Galatians 5. By way of comparison to the fruit of the Spirit, in these texts Paul presents lists of works of the flesh. These include such behaviors as picking fights, insisting on your own way, fornication, jealousy, slander, malice, envy, drunkenness and carousing. All these "fruit of the flesh" are activities people do outside themselves, usually involving others. While people who fornicate, fight or carouse may do it with feeling, emotion is only a part of the action.

In the same way, the fruit of the Spirit must also be understood as behaviors and actions. Love, for example, does not simply mean being attracted or feeling warmly toward another. It also means expressing affection and doing things loved ones will appreciate. Things like unexpectedly

peace, patience, kindness, goodness, faithfulness, gentleness and self-control. I don't think we realize how practical these fruit of the Spirit are. We imagine that they are good feelings, but they really are principles of good conduct.

Paul describes the fruit of the Spirit as divinely prompted antidotes for our bad behaviors (see Gal 5:16-25). Patience, for example corrects anger by helping us to direct that adrenalin-driven emotion into some constructive action. Kindness overrides our mean streaks and motivates us to serve others with unexpected generosity. Peace calms our fighting and gets us to

---

doing one of their chores, avoiding actions that irk them and listening carefully when they are speaking.

Colossians 3 and Galatians 5 also help us dispel misconceptions about the fruit of the Spirit. We may mistakenly imagine that they are nice, positive qualities that God deposits in us. We may even think of them as somewhat passive virtues nestled in among our nastier qualities, where they may be jostled, bruised and beaten down.

In reality, the fruit of the Spirit are not namby-pamby graces that cower in the presence of such menaces as envy, lust or hatred. Faced with the works of the flesh, the fruit of the Spirit do not go for coexistence. They are after conquest. Paul says that all who belong to Christ have crucified the old self with all of its passions and desires (see Gal 5:24). So the fruit of the Spirit are not a polite veneer of niceness that conceals our badness, giving the false impression that we are like Christ. Instead, they are strong, aggressive resources that defang our evil tendencies. When they've done their work we really become like Jesus from the inside out.

Adapted from Bert Ghezzi, *Becoming More Like Jesus*, 16–18.

resolve the causes of our conflicts. And so on.

All of these behaviors improve the way we relate to others. If I let the Holy Spirit work in me, for example, I may be able to do something good for a person I don't like very much. Or he may inspire me to give generously to a person in need, even when I am feeling stingy. So the fruit of the Spirit is the substance of real love.

Producing the fruit of the Spirit in us is mainly the work of the Holy Spirit, but we must do our part. We must pray and we must choose. First, we need to ask the Spirit to work with our problem tendencies, giving him permission to prompt us to good behavior when we feel like being bad. I think it's wise to start each day by inviting the Spirit to roam through our lives inspiring wholesome conduct.

Second, we must choose to act differently when we feel inclined to behave badly. Easier said than done, you say? I agree that changing persistently negative behavior is hard. But change we must, and the Holy Spirit is with us to make it possible. "Live according to your new life in the Spirit," advises Paul. "Then you won't be doing what your sinful nature craves" (Gal 5:16, NLT). When you and I are speaking and acting more Christianly, we will become signs of real love. Everyone around us will notice because they will feel its benefits.

FOR REFLECTION AND DISCUSSION

1. Why do you think Scripture and the Church make love of others a measure of our love of God?

2. Why do we find it difficult to do the loving thing in our relationships?

3. What are the fruit of the Spirit? How do they act as antidotes for evil inclinations and actions?

4. What do the fruit of the Spirit have to do with relationships?

5. How do we acquire the fruit of the Spirit?

6. What is the condition of my personal relationships? What one thing might I do to improve them?

ACTION IDEAS

1. Think about your family, friends, neighbors and colleagues. Is there someone among them with whom you have a difficult relationship? For the next month pray for your relationship with that person. Invite the Holy Spirit to bring to mind what you must do or how you must change so that the relationship can improve.

2. Read and reflect on Galatians 5:16-25. Ask these questions: What was Paul saying in these texts? What is the Spirit saying to me through his words today? Look for one action you could do to replace a bad behavior with a good one. Pray for the Holy Spirit's help.

3. Study Colossians 3:5-15 (see box on pp. 114–15). Has someone hurt you whom you have not forgiven? Ask the Holy Spirit to give you the strength to forgive that person. If he or she asks for forgiveness, grant it freely. However, if the person has not approached you, forgive him or her unilaterally in your heart. Do not say anything to the person and expect nothing of them.

R E A D   M E !

- Edward D. O'Connor, C.S.C., *The Catholic Vision* (Our Sunday Visitor: 800-348-2440), 357–62.

- Alan Schreck, *Hearts Aflame: The Holy Spirit at the Heart of Christian Life Today* (Servant Publications: 734-677-6490), 89–108.

THIRTEEN

Going to Confession

I always have liked going to confession. You may find that a bit unusual, especially if it doesn't match your experience. Oh, yes, sometimes I am nervous or ashamed as I wait in line for my turn. But those uncomfortable feelings seem less bothersome than the load of guilt I carry because of some unresolved wrongdoing. Before confessing, my life looks to me like an unmade bed. Afterward, however, it feels like a freshly made-up bed, with clean sheets neatly tucked in hospital corners, and a mint on the pillow. Very nice, indeed.

The need to confess sins was indelibly impressed on me in my childhood. I attended Catholic schools in the 1940s and '50s. From second grade on, every month the sisters routinely marched us to church for confession. We learned about such things as examining our conscience, distinguishing mortal from venial sins and avoiding the near occasions of sin. All this was habit-forming. Thus, my early experience still shapes my approach to the sacrament of reconciliation, even though much about the way we do it has changed in the last thirty years.

When I was a kid, we anonymously confessed laundry lists of sins to a priest hidden behind a screen. Receiving the sacrament was very formal, pretty much scripted from the "Bless me, Father" at the start to the Act of Contrition at the finish. The focus seemed to be on getting absolution for your sins. Today, going to confession is less formal. Ever since the rite of the sacrament was reformed in 1973, we normally confess to a priest face-to-face.

HOW WE GO
TO CONFESSION

The Church now provides three rites for celebrating the sacrament of reconciliation:

For Individual Penitents. Although we still have the option of confessing with a screen between ourselves and the priest, we are encouraged to meet the celebrant face-to-face whenever possible. When we first enter the reconciliation room, the priest greets us in the name of Christ and we return the greeting. A passage of Scripture chosen by us or the priest is then read.

We confess our sins in the form of a conversation with the priest about our sins. In particular, we are encouraged to discuss sinful or selfish patterns in our lives out of which our sin emerges. Together we discuss ways to overcome our sins and our sinful behavior patterns. This rite invites us to reflect about why we do the things we do, and how we might change.

The telling of sins ends when we ask the celebrant for our penance and for the blessing of absolution. The priest will ask us to say a particular prayer or to do a particular action as a sign of our sorrow. He may ask us to say an "Act of Contrition," either from a card, from memory or spontaneously (see box on p. 124).

Finally, the priest extends his hands over us and says the prayers of absolution to grant us forgiveness in the name of

God and of our church community. The rite ends with sharing a greeting of peace or a handshake.

For Several Penitents With Individual Confession, commonly called a "communal penance service." In this rite, the greeting, Scripture and "Act of Contrition" are done together, like a mini-version of the Liturgy of the Word at Mass. Then we approach a priest individually to tell our sins in a conversational manner and receive absolution. The celebrant will either give us a penance or give a penance to all participants at the same time after all have confessed. The ritual often ends with a closing prayer and a song.

For Several Penitents With Confession, commonly called "General Absolution." There are many restrictions on when this rite may be used. It is intended for special and unusual circumstances such as an emergency that requires absolution be given quickly to a large group. This rite, too, includes public prayers and Scripture readings. We do not confess sins aloud, but we acknowledge our sinfulness with prayer or gestures such as kneeling or bowing. The words of absolution, offered to all present, are prayed aloud over the whole community at once. Anyone who has committed a serious sin is expected to confess individually to a priest.

Adapted from Peg Bowman, *At Home with the Sacraments: Reconciliation* (Twenty-Third Publications: 800-321-0411), 30–32.

The contemporary rite is loosely structured and unscripted. The focus is less on getting absolved of a specific list of sins and more on receiving forgiveness, healing and counsel for sinful patterns that mar our lives.

While the rite has changed, however, the substance of the sacrament of reconciliation and Catholic teaching about it have not. Neither has sin changed. We need the sacrament of reconciliation now as much as we ever did.

Today, however, the majority of Catholics rarely make use of it. Some attend communal penance services during Advent and Lent; only a few confess more frequently; and most, I think, don't go to confession at all. Many reasons account for this. Some of us abandoned the sacrament because of a bad experience in the confessional. Or we gave up on it because our rattling off a list of sins seemed meaningless and unhelpful. Some are simply uninformed and don't approach the sacrament because their religious education was incomplete.

On the positive side, I think many Catholics attend the sacrament less often because they have learned to practice repentance in their daily lives. And they take advantage of the reconciliation service at every Mass to get square with God and the community. On the whole, we seem to have a greater appreciation of God's mercy than earlier generations of Catholics that focused on his judgment. That's a healthy attitude adjustment, don't you think? But perhaps we have overcorrected. An occasional thought about fire and brimstone might serve us well.

Many contemporary Catholics seem to have lost awareness of the seriousness of sin. That, I think, is the main reason we don't go to confession. We have become casual about wrongdoing, pretending that sinful behavior has no consequences. Our culture relentlessly presses us into its amoral and immoral molds. We often find it easier to conform to its lax standards than to measure ourselves against God's standards—the Ten Commandments and the laws of love. Gradually, we make ourselves comfortable with our sins, treating them as old friends instead of as the foes they really are. Thus, we don't feel much need for confession.

We must face the fact that sin is our lethal enemy. A noxious spiritual virus, serious sin has the toxic power to destroy our relationship with God and cut us off from the Christian community. Ultimately, it may annihilate our souls. For good reason our ancestors spoke of some sins as a "deadly" seven: pride, greed, rage, lust, envy, sloth and gluttony. We would be wise to cultivate a similar perspective on grievous wrongdoing. A robust fear of such sins would motivate us to avoid them and to frequent the sacrament of reconciliation for help in fighting them.

The *Catechism of the Catholic Church* (#1470) says that when we go to confession we anticipate our judgment before God after our death. I find that thought both encouraging and sobering. Encouraging, because confession is no mere dry run, but a real foretaste of the merciful justice I can expect from God when I come before him in his heavenly court.

But it is also a sobering idea because even a hint of death highlights the potentially dangerous consequences of sin and prompts me to repent. To heighten my own realization of the imminence of judgment, I often repeat these words of St. Thomas More: "Death stealeth on full slyly; unaware, he lies at hand and shall us all surprise, we know not when, nor where nor in what wise." This verse sends me running into the arms of a loving Father, who always says yes to my pleas for mercy.

We call the sacrament of confession by other names that show it's not just about telling our sins and seeking forgiveness for them. Most often since Vatican II we have referred to it as "reconciliation." As the term suggests, the sacrament restores and builds our relationship with God, which we may have broken by some wrongdoing.

Reconciliation also heals any damage our sin may have done to the Christian community. This means that sin and the sacrament are not matters between me and God, reserved for the confessional. Most sins involve others, hurting them by something we say, do or omit. Lies, gossip, rage, snobbery, infidelity, cheating and a host of other evil actions injure the people around us. The sacrament of reconciliation not only supplies forgiveness for our deeds, but it also gives us the grace to fix the brokenness we may have caused. Thus, the sacrament is not just about confessing sins. It is about loving others, and so reaches into our daily lives.

We also call confession the "sacrament of penance," which is its most ancient name. The term *penance* focuses us on the reform of our lives and on our growth in holiness. Penance is an opportunity

---

AN ACT OF CONTRITION

My God,
I am sorry for my sins with all my heart.
In choosing to do wrong and failing to do good
I have sinned against you
whom I should love above all things.
I firmly intend, with your help,
to do penance,
to sin no more
and to avoid whatever leads me to sin.

Revised Rite of Penance

for us to identify the faults and sinful patterns in our lives, to get advice about dealing with them, and to receive healing for them and the spiritual strength to transform them. We meet Jesus in the sacrament. There he helps us turn our anger into patience, our greed into generosity, our pride into humility and so on. Thus, penance is really about becoming more like Christ.

So here I am waiting my turn to go into the reconciliation room and confess to Fr. Ed. I feel a twinge of nervousness, but then I remind myself that Jesus will be there, too. Nothing to be afraid of, for he is not only my Judge, but he is my Savior, who chose to die a savage death to forgive the sins I am about to tell.

FOR REFLECTION AND DISCUSSION

1. Why do we need the sacrament of confession?

2. Why do you think we have lost a sense of the seriousness of sin? What are the consequences of serious sins?

3. In what way does going to confession anticipate our judgment before God after death?

4. The sacrament of confession is now commonly called reconciliation. What truths about the sacrament does that name suggest?

5. The sacrament of confession is also called penance. What realities about the sacrament does that name suggest?

ACTION IDEAS

1. If you are baptized and have not yet participated in the sacrament of reconciliation, ask your pastor or someone on your parish staff to arrange for your first confession.

2. Set aside a block of time—at least an hour—to review your life, looking both for patterns of behavior that please God and for patterns that lead you to sin. When you have completed your survey, take a brief time to pray. Thank God for prompting your good actions. Tell him you are sorry for your sins. At the next opportunity, go to confession.

3. If your parish offers a communal penance service, go to the next one. Invite family or friends to attend with you. Participate fully in all parts of the service.

R E A D   M E !

- The *Catechism of the Catholic Church* (#1422–98) summarizes Catholic teaching on the sacrament of reconciliation.

- Peg Bowman, *At Home with the Sacraments: Reconciliation* (Twenty-Third Publications: 800-321-0411) is a short, popular discussion of the sacrament.

- Bert Ghezzi, *50 Ways to Tap the Power of the Sacraments* (Our Sunday Visitor: 800-348-2440) discusses practical ways of building confession and reconciliation into daily life.

Reaching Beyond Ourselves

"We may not think of ourselves as being very significant in God's scheme of things. But we are. Christ gives us as his disciples important roles to play in continuing his work among human beings. He gives us all "a piece of the action." For today he reaches people through us. He speaks with our voices, embraces with our arms, heals with our touch, and goes to aid people with our feet."

FOURTEEN

The Parish—Our Christian Family

Over the years Mary Lou and I have lived in eight different parishes in five cities. Each parish community was unique, having its own personality and style. In some of these parishes we flourished, but in others we didn't. What made the difference? Why did we thrive in some parishes and languish in others? Was it the pastor? The congregation? The liturgy? The youth program? These may have been factors, but looking back I think I can put my finger on the real reason. It was *us*. The more active we were in the parish, the more life we found there. When we were only marginally involved, our Christian experience was the poorer for it.

I am not surprised that our family did not do so well when we tried to go it alone. The Church as Christ founded it is not individualistic. It's not "me and God." No, he made it corporate. It's "me and others in God." Of course, we have a personal relationship with God and must spend time alone with him. But the Lord designed the Church to be a community and intends us to find life and love among the people there.

Jesus himself was never a "loner." From the outset of his ministry, he surrounded himself with people. An entourage of loyal men and women accompanied him as he carried his message from village to village. Christ formed these early followers into an informal community of believers. He gathered them around himself in a series of widening circles: Peter, James and John; the Twelve; the Seventy-Two and beyond these, a larger group of disciples. Jesus was laying the groundwork for the Church, assembling the women and men he would bring into God's family.

Establishing God's family on planet Earth is what Jesus was about. All who believed in him he made sons and daughters of God (see Jn 1:12). That's the origin of the Church, the extended divine family, which now includes latecomers like you and me. As children of the same Father, we became brothers and sisters to Christ and to each other. That's why Jesus taught us to pray the "*Our* Father." And that's what he meant after the resurrection when he directed Mary Magdalene to tell his disciples: "I am ascending to my Father and *your* Father, to my God and *your* God" (Jn 20:17, emphasis added).

Today the Church may not feel like a family to us. Its sheer size requires a governmental structure that may seem to be impersonal and bureaucratic. But beneath the Catholic Church's worldwide organization of national conferences, dioceses and parishes is the community Christ founded. Our parish is a local branch of that divine family. And to be fully Catholic we must participate in its life.

The next time you're at Mass, take a look around. These people who are worshiping with you—many of them probably strangers—are your brothers and sisters. We are actually closer to them than we may realize, since the link that binds us is the Holy Spirit himself.

Our brotherhood in Christ, real as it is, remains underdeveloped—even latent—unless we take action to bring it to life. Making friends of some fellow parishioners is the main thing we can do. I learned this firsthand many years ago.

A job change moved my family to a new town. We joined St. Charles, the local parish, which seemed to have more than its share of problems. Some people were disgruntled because the school had been closed. Parishioners were divided over the liturgical

CHRISTIAN FRIENDSHIP

As the Father has loved me, so have I loved you; abide in my love. If you keep my commandments, you will abide in my love, just as I have kept my Father's commandments and abide in his love. These things I have spoken to you, that my joy may be in you, and that your joy may be full.

This is my commandment, that you love one another as I have loved you. Greater love has no man than this, that a man lay down his life for his friends. You are my friends if you do what I command you. No longer do I call you servants, for the servant does not know what his master is doing; but I have called you friends, for all that I have heard from my Father I have made known to you. You did not choose me, but I chose you that you should go and bear fruit and that your fruit should abide; so that whatever you ask the Father in my name, he may give it to you. This I command you, to love one another.

JOHN 15:9-17

changes. The pastor was overworked and ready to retire, and so on. The place seemed tense, unhappy and even moribund.

Shortly after we signed up, however, a young couple came to our house to welcome us. They invited Mary Lou and me to join with them and a few other couples who were getting together the following week. We took them up on it, enjoyed the camaraderie, and the next month invited the group to our home. In a short time these men and women became our friends and these new relationships changed our perspective on the parish. While the problems did not magically disappear, we no longer felt like we were part of a dying organization. Making friends transformed our experience by focusing us on knowing and loving our sisters and brothers.

Looking for ways to serve people is another way to help our parish become more of the family it's supposed to be. To do this we may have to change our thought patterns. Experience has trained us always to ask, What's in it for me? A perfectly good and reasonable question to test many opportunities that come our way. But it's not the right question to test our parish involvement. The people there are our Christian family, and we should be asking

---

THE FAMILY OF GOD

From the beginning of salvation history [God] has chosen men not just as individuals but as members of a certain community. Revealing His mind to them, God called these chosen ones "His people" (Ex 3:7-12), and even made a covenant with them on Sinai.

This communitarian character is developed and consummated in the work of Jesus Christ. For the very Word made flesh willed to share in the human fellowship. He was present at the wedding of Cana, visited the house of Zacchaeus, ate with publicans and sinners. He revealed the love of the Father and the sublime vocation of man in terms of the most common social realities and by making use of the speech and the imagery of plain everyday life....

In His preaching He clearly taught the sons of God to treat one another as brothers. In His prayers He pleaded that all His disciples might be "one." Indeed, as the redeemer of all, He offered Himself for all even to point of

ourselves, What can I give of myself to my brothers and sisters?

Mary Lou and I, for example, began to value St. Charles Parish more once we plunged in and began to participate actively. Mary Lou got elected to St. Charles' first parish council. There she was able to contribute significantly to the parish's effort to implement the vision of Vatican II. I served as a lector and helped a few others learn to read Scripture at Mass. Our volunteering made things a little better for the parish and a lot better for us.

So make friends of people in your parish. Look for ways to serve and do it generously. Work at it. But remember that these activities are not merely techniques to improve our experience of parish life.

---

death. "Greater love has no man than this, that a man lay down his life for his friends" (Jn 15:13). He commanded His Apostles to preach to all peoples the gospel's message that the human race was to become the Family of God, in which the fullness of the Law would be love.

As the first-born of many brethren and by the giving of His Spirit, He founded after His death and resurrection a new brotherly community composed of all those who receive Him in faith and in love. This He did through His Body, which is the Church. There everyone, as members one of the other, would render mutual service according to the different gifts bestowed on each.

This solidarity must be constantly increased until that day on which it will be brought to perfection. Then, saved by grace, man will offer flawless glory to God as a family beloved of God and of Christ their Brother.

Vatican Council II, *Pastoral Constitution on the Church in the Modern World [Gaudium et Spes]*, 32.

They are normal ways of expressing love among brothers and sisters, as essential to the parish community as they are in the life of any human family.

FOR REFLECTION AND DISCUSSION

1. Why did Jesus surround himself with a community of disciples?

2. What does it mean to you that as a Christian you are part of God's family?

3. Why must we work at building community relationships in our parishes?

4. What do you think is the single most important thing you can do to become more a part of the local Christian community?

ACTION IDEAS

1. During the next six months participate as much as possible in your parish's social activities. Take friends or family with you to breakfasts, picnics and the like, but be sure to meet new people at these events. If you have an opportunity to serve at some function, do it as a way of making friends of sisters and brothers in your parish community.

2. Once a month for the next six months, invite a few people to come to your home after Sunday Mass for a simple breakfast. Let people who offer bring something to share.

3. Survey service options available in your parish. Select one that interests you, and investigate what it might take for you to participate in it. If it suits you, involve yourself with the group.

Your purpose should be twofold: to serve others and to make friends.

READ ME!

- Archbishop Daniel E. Pilarczyk, *The Parish: Where God's People Live* (Paulist Press: 800-218-1903).

FIFTEEN

Making Friends for Christ and the Church

When my family moved to Florida, our new evangelical neighbors warmly welcomed us. To make us feel at home, they brought us meals. They invited us to join them at church-sponsored family activities. Once my son went with a buddy to a service at their church, an event which triggered a whole stream of invitations. The affable youth pastor began to phone him frequently.

Finally, one evening I answered a knock at the door. With a broad smile and firm handshake, the senior pastor himself greeted me and asked if he could visit. He wanted Mary Lou and me to encourage our son to attend his church. I heroically resisted the temptation to introduce myself as the author of *Keeping Your Kids Catholic* and to hand him an autographed copy of my book. Instead, I praised him and his congregation for their generous efforts to attract us to their church. But I politely asked him to stop pursuing my son. I explained that we, like him, loved Christ and the gospel and that we were living our faith as deeply committed Catholics.

My intervention ended the friendly invasion. But I can't help thinking that had we been less solidly Catholic, the genuine concern and affection of these outgoing Christians would have drawn us to their church.

What do you think motivated their outreach to my family? Were they merely recruiting people to swell their congregation? Maybe. Or were they trying to "save" us, misguided by a false notion that

Catholics are not Christians? Perhaps that was the case, but they never said as much. Even if that were so, the warmth and dedication of their approaches to us would have caused me to forgive— and gently correct—their error.

In their minds, I'm sure, my neighbors regarded their activities as "evangelism." Or as Catholics say, "evangelization." They believed they were doing their part to fulfill Jesus' Great Commission "to make disciples of all nations" (see Mt 28:19-20). I'm convinced that Catholics have much to learn from folks like these. When Jesus charged his followers to make disciples of others, to bring them to baptism and to teach them to observe his commandments, he was also talking to us. To the community that would be called the Catholic Church. To you and to me.

Spreading the faith is not the prerogative of a few professional missionaries. Evangelization is the privilege and duty of every baptized person. "No believer in Christ," says Pope John Paul II, "can avoid this supreme duty: to proclaim Christ to all peoples."[1] We dare not avoid the matter. There's no way around it. Doing evangelism is Christ's command, echoed in the Church. So what are we doing about it?

Evangelization has many modes, some of which are specialized and not for all. For example, conducting mass rallies, preaching on street corners or canvasing neighborhoods require unique callings and gifts. But the kind of evangelization my neighbors do is for everyone. They were doing "friendship evangelism," something that each of us can accomplish every day.

Make friends, and then help them become friends with Christ. That's all there is to friendship evangelization. No graduate education required, no technical training needed. Just conduct our daily affairs and relationships in a manner that opens people to God. We can all be "friendship evangelists" by behaving and speaking in

EVANGELIZATION—
WITNESS AND WORD

Above all, the Gospel must be proclaimed by witness. Take a Christian or a handful of Christians who, in the midst of their own community, show their capacity for understanding and acceptance, their sharing of life and destiny with other people, their solidarity with efforts of all for whatever is noble and good. Let us suppose that, in addition, they radiate in an altogether simple and unaffected way their faith in values that go beyond current values, and their hope in something that is not seen and that one would not dare to imagine. Through this wordless witness these Christians stir up irresistible questions in the hearts of those who see how they live: Why are they like this? Why do they live in this way? What or who is it that inspires them? ... Such a witness is already a silent proclamation of the Good News and a very powerful and effective one.

Nevertheless this always remains insufficient because even the finest witness will prove ineffective in the long run if it is not explained, justified—what Peter called always having "your answer ready for people who ask you the reason for the hope that you all have" (see 1 Pt 3:15)—and made explicit by a clear and unequivocal proclamation of the Lord Jesus. The Good News proclaimed by the witness of life sooner or later has to be proclaimed by the word of life. There is no true evangelization if the name, the teaching, the life, the promises, the Kingdom and the mystery of Jesus of Nazareth, the son of God are not proclaimed.

Pope Paul VI, *Evangelization in the Modern World [Evangelii Nuntiandi]*, 21–22.

ways that draw others to Christ and the Church.

Consider these snapshots of Catholics doing friendship evangelization:

- Once a month Minnie packs up her china tea set and holds a tea party for eight elderly women in a nearby assisted-living center. The ladies love to talk to Minnie because she is a good listener. When they give her an opening, she speaks simply about what Christ has done for her and about his love for them.

- Greg is a team leader in a technology company. He shows remarkable patience in frustrating circumstances. When the group goes drinking he orders a Coke. Occasionally, someone asks why he doesn't blow up or why he doesn't drink. Then Greg explains his lifelong struggles against anger and alcohol, and tells how receiving Christ in the Eucharist has helped him get control of himself.

- Once Veronica, a student, asked Paul, her professor, if she could have an hour of his time to make a presentation about network marketing. Paul agreed on condition that she would give him an hour to explain why he was a follower of Christ and a member of the Catholic Church. She was trying to recruit him into her pyramid. He was trying to draw her to the Lord.

- The company where Annette works as a manager is downsizing, and her colleagues are afraid for their jobs. At meetings and in personal conversations, Annette uses humor and encouragement to give people hope. Many have asked her how she stays so upbeat, and she talks about her faith and urges them to trust God. She has even prayed with people at work.

Notice in these examples that friendship evangelization involves both *show* and *tell*. Our behavior must be openly Christlike so as to intrigue others. That's the "show." As Pope Paul VI said in his

THE URGENCY OF EVANGELIZATION

The number of those awaiting Christ is still immense. The human and cultural groups not yet reached by the Gospel or for whom the Church is scarcely present are so widespread as to require the uniting of all the Church's resources. As she prepares to celebrate the jubilee of the year 2000, the whole Church is even more committed to a new missionary advent. We must increase our apostolic zeal to pass on to others the light and joy of the faith, and to this high ideal the whole people of God must be educated.

We cannot be content when we consider the millions of our brothers and sisters who, like us, have been redeemed by the blood of Christ, but who live in ignorance of the love of God. For each believer, as for the entire Church, the missionary task must remain foremost, for it concerns the eternal destiny of humanity and corresponds to God's mysterious and merciful plan.

Pope John Paul II, *The Mission of the Redeemer [Redemptoris Missio]*, 86.

remarkable encyclical *On Evangelization in the Modern World*, we want to stir up irresistible questions in people's hearts: Why are they like this? Who is it that inspires them? Our witness opens people up. (An encyclical, by the way, is a letter which a pope writes to the Church and the world.)

But, of course, example alone will never be enough to bring people to Christ. There must always be a "tell." "Even the finest witness," said Pope Paul VI, "will prove ineffective in the long run if it is not explained, justified.... The Good News proclaimed by the witness of life sooner or later has to be proclaimed by the word of life" (see box on p. 139). We must be ready to explain in our own words what we believe and why. Nothing fancy. Just what comes from our hearts, as Minnie does with her lady friends and Greg with his team.

We can make some decisions to help us get in the habit of making friends for Christ and the Church:

First, we must be deliberate about it. We must make a decision to do the show and tell that friendship evangelization requires.

Second, we must pray for the people in all of our circles—family, friends, neighbors, colleagues and so on. The Evangelizer who does most of the work is the Holy Spirit; we are only his helpers. Prayer is perhaps our main contribution to the effort, taking first place even ahead of show and tell.

Third, we must be on the watch for opportunities to do or say something that will nudge a friend a little closer to Christ.

You know, I have an idea. A new family just moved in across the street. I think I'll get Mary Lou, and we'll go over to welcome them. We can invite them to go with us to our parish social next weekend. Who knows what that might lead to?

FOR REFLECTION AND DISCUSSION

1. What is "friendship" evangelization?

2. Why must evangelization involve both *show* and *tell?*

3. Have I ever helped a relative or friend get closer to Christ? What happened?

4. What one thing could I do differently to help others find Christ and the Church?

ACTION IDEAS

1. For the next three months pray daily for the people you associate with regularly. For example, your family or the people you live with; work or school colleagues; people you serve with at church; those you recreate with; your car pool; clerks at stores you patronize, and so on. Pray specifically for them—for salvation, sanctification, greater knowledge of Christ and coming to his Church. Watch for opportunities to say or do something that draws them nearer to Christ. And do it. At the end of three months, review your experience. Then do it again.

2. For the next month, experiment with friendship evangelism in your family or living situation. Pray daily for each person. Consider what kindnesses in word or action you might do to serve each one. Ask yourself what you could do differently that might prompt a family member or friend to open more to God. For example, a man once "evangelized" his wife by starting to take out the garbage without her having to nag him. When she asked what had gotten into him, he told her simply about his recent experience of coming to know the love of Christ.

3. Take some time to prepare what you might say when someone asks you about your faith in Christ and the Church. Ask yourself questions like the following: How did I come to know Christ? Why am I a member of the Catholic Church? What has Christ done for me? How do I experience life in the Church? What can I say to someone to help them put faith in Christ and the Church? Reflecting on these subjects will create a reservoir you

can draw on when you have an opportunity to speak to someone about your faith.

R E A D   M E !

- *The Mission of the Redeemer [Redemptoris Missio],* encyclical let-
ter of Pope John Paul II, and *Evangelization in the Modern
World [Evangelii Nuntiandi],* encyclical letter of Pope Paul VI
are basic reading for all Catholics. For copies write to the
Publications Office, United States Catholic Conference, 1312
Massachusetts Avenue N. W., Washington, D.C. 20002 or call
Pauline Books & Media (800-876-4463).

- Bert Ghezzi, *Sharing Your Faith: A User's Guide to Evangelization* (Our Sunday Visitor: 800-348-2440) introduces
Catholics to friendship evangelization.

SIXTEEN

Christian Service—Our Piece of Christ's Action

A mong all the names for the Church—People of God, House of God, Family of God, Bride of Christ—one of my favorites is the Body of Christ. That's because my discovering its meaning as a college sophomore was mind-blowing. I remember well how it happened. A professor had me read Pope Pius XII's encyclical *On the Mystical Body of Christ*. As a young man I found papal documents hard to read. Even though they were in English, they still seemed to be in a language foreign to me. But not that one. Pope Pius XII's letter opened my eyes to the reality of the Church.

At the time I had a very limited understanding of the Church. Like many Catholics of that day, I saw it as God's house, the building where we gathered for Mass. I also thought of it as an international organization of parishes. My view was not false, just incomplete. Pope Pius XII startled me by describing the Church as a living organism, the body of Christ. The pope was not using a metaphor or an analogy here. He was declaring a fact. He said the Church *is* the body of Christ. He sent me scurrying to the Bible to learn more about it. There I found that Paul had stated it plainly in 1 Corinthians 12: *"Now you are the body of Christ and individually members of it"* (verse 27). Absorbing that truth deepened my relationship to Christ because I perceived the Church more accurately.

Reading the encyclical caused me to look at other believers differently. Before I saw myself as one of many members in a religious organization. Being Catholic meant we went to Mass on Sundays, obeyed the commandments, took direction from priests and religious, contributed to the support of the parish and so on. After reading the pope's letter, I realized that there was more to it—that I was a unique cell linked by the Holy Spirit to many others in Christ's corporate body. Being Catholic came to mean living in Christ and sharing the same life with all Christians.

Jesus came to earth as one of us, conducting his ministry of preaching, teaching and healing through his human body. While he achieved a universal salvation through his death and resurrection,

---

HOW THE BODY OF CHRIST WORKS

For by the grace given to me I tell everyone among you not to think of himself more highly than one ought to think, but to think soberly, each according to the measure of faith that God has apportioned. For as in one body we have many parts, and all the parts do not have the same function, so we, though many, are one body in Christ and individually parts of one another.

Since we have gifts that differ according to the grace given to us, let us exercise them: if prophecy, in proportion to the faith; if ministry, in ministering; if one is a teacher, in teaching; if one exhorts, in exhortation; if one contributes, in generosity; if one is over others, with diligence; if one does acts of mercy, with cheerfulness.

Let love be sincere; hate what is evil, hold on to what is good; love one another with mutual affection; anticipate one another in showing honor. Do not grow slack in zeal, be fervent in spirit, serve the Lord.

ROMANS 12:3-11 (NAB)

the physical limits of his body restricted his personal ministry. For example, he had to walk wherever he went, traversing only a few thousand square miles during his public ministry. And five thousand may have been the largest crowd he ever spoke to. However, Jesus has become a corporate body, the Church, of which he is the head and millions of us are his members. As a result, now Christ's outreach is global and potentially unrestricted. Since we are the agents commissioned to carry on his work in the world, our ignorance and selfishness are the only limits on his ministry.

We may not think of ourselves as being very significant in God's scheme of things. But we are. Christ gives us as his disciples important roles to play in continuing his work among human beings. He gives us all "a piece of the action." For today he reaches people through us. He speaks with our voices, embraces with our arms, heals with our touch, goes to aid people with our feet and so on.

Here's how it works. All baptized persons receive gifts from the Holy Spirit. These equip us to perform specific services for others in the Church and the world. Just as the life and health of a human body depend on every member doing its part, so too with the body of Christ. I use my gifts to serve you. You use your gifts to serve me. Love and interdependence flow from this exchange. Thus, the body of Christ thrives in good health and can achieve the Lord's purposes on the earth.

Christ's gifts come in great diversity, each one making some essential contribution to the life of the body. You will find numerous examples listed in the New Testament (see Rom 12:6-8; 1 Cor 12:4-11; Eph 4:11-12; 1 Pt 4:9-11). But these lists are deliberately incomplete and are meant to suggest the vast variety of gifts. Some gifts, like teaching and healing, are public. Others operate mainly behind the scenes, for example, administrating programs and contributing money. Gifts like miracles are spectacular, but others like faith and giving encouragement do not attract much attention.

Take a look at the following Catholics and their gifts. Notice some things about all of them. Their gifts are practical, benefiting others materially and spiritually. And their gifts equip them for service, enabling them to act in ways that strengthen the Church and reach out to others in their society.

- George is affectionate, a good listener and knows how to speak personally and simply about the Christian life. He participates in a ministry to prisoners, using his gifts to win men to Christ, to counsel them and to instruct them in the fundamentals of the faith.

- Hospitality is Madeleine's gift. She makes guests feel right at home, and somehow they always feel better off for having been with her.

- Mary is a consummate administrator; sometimes I think she could run the United Nations. For thirty years she has organized events and programs in her parish and town.

- No one I know can make the Bible come alive for others like Fr. Ed. His gift is an ability to penetrate the meaning of God's Word and communicate it in attention-getting ways.

- Mary Lou, a librarian, uses her professional expertise and her singular compassion to choose just the right books to cheer the homebound sick and elderly whom she visits each week.

- Every year a local parish cooperates with Habitat for Humanity to build a house for a needy family. Joe uses his gifts as an engineer, manager and handyman to lead the construction team.

- Sharon is a news anchor at a local T.V. station. She uses her gift of speech as a lector at Mass, and she also trains others to read Scripture well.

- Mara and Gene serve as sponsors for candidates in their parish's RCIA program. They seem to be able to support and coach people in the important personal decisions they must make as they join the Church.

- Grace is an invalid, but she spends at least an hour a day interceding for her family and friends. On her nightstand she keeps a little notebook to record answered prayers, and it's almost full.

THE BODY OF CHRIST DEPENDS ON US

The Church was founded for the purpose of spreading the kingdom of Christ throughout the earth for the glory of God the Father, to enable all men to share in His saving redemption, and that through them the whole world might enter into a relationship with Christ. All activity of the Mystical Body directed to the attainment of this goal is called the apostolate, which the Church carries on in various ways through all her members. For the Christian vocation by its very nature is also a vocation to the apostolate. No part of the structure of a living body is merely passive but has a share in the functions as well as life of the body: so, too, in the body of Christ, which is the Church, the whole body, "according to the functioning in due measure of each single part, derives its increase" (Eph 4:16).

Indeed, the organic union in this body and the structure of the members are so compact that the member who fails to make his proper contribution to the development of the Church must be said to be useful neither to the Church nor to himself.

Vatican Council II, *Decree on the Apostolate of the Laity [Apostolicam Actuositatem]*, 2.

You might think that some of these gifts don't seem very "spiritual." For example, organizing programs, delivering books to the homebound or building houses. But all these services, even those which seem most mundane or material, are truly spiritual. What makes them so is that they are inspired and directed by the Holy Spirit.

So, you ask, how do I discover what my gifts are? How do I find out how I am supposed to serve in the body of Christ? Well, don't look too hard at yourself or you might get paralyzed by self-absorption. Rather, look around you to see what needs to be done and figure out what part you can play in making it happen. Is one of my neighbors in need? How can I help? Can I do something to meet a need in my parish community? How do I volunteer? We learn by doing what our gifts are. By plunging in and serving we learn what our service is. If we don't notice what we do best, we can count on others to tell us. That's how we get our piece of Christ's action.

FOR REFLECTION AND DISCUSSION

1. What do you think it means to say that the Church *is* the body of Christ?

2. How does being the body of Christ make the Church different from every other human institution?

3. How does the Church continue Jesus' ministry? In what sense is Christ's ministry now less restricted and more global than when he walked the earth?

4. Why do you think Christ gives gifts to every baptized Christian?

5. What makes gifts of service "spiritual"?

6. How do you find your service in the body of Christ?

A C T I O N   I D E A S

1. Study the Scripture texts about service in the body of Christ (see Rom 12:1-21; 1 Cor 12:1-31, 13:1-13; Eph 4:1-15; 1 Pt 4:7-11). Make it your goal to understand what the writer was trying to say, as well as what the Spirit is saying today to you through the text. Look for one thing you might do differently to use your gifts more effectively in the Church and the world.

2. Write a list of all the things you think you do well. Ask the Holy Spirit for guidance. For example, one person might include the following activities: write good letters; give clear directions; organize personal stuff; make others laugh. Then consider how you can use these abilities in the service of Christ and the Church. For instance, perhaps the person who writes good letters and makes others laugh should look for ways of corresponding to people, giving them hope and encouragement for Christian living.

3. If you are already serving in some way, invite the Holy Spirit to help you use your gifts more lovingly and with greater effect. Consider praying daily the "Come, Holy Spirit" (see box on p. 74) or the "Hymn to the Holy Spirit" (see box on p. 98). Figure out a way to observe the results of your prayer. For example, pick two days in the near future, say six months and a year down the road; mark them on your calendar. Take an hour on each of those days to review how you have served and what fruit your gifts have produced.

READ ME!

- Vatican Council II, *Decree on the Apostolate of the Laity [Apostolicam Actuositatem]* (Pauline Books and Media: 800-876-4463).

- Pope Pius XI, *On the Mystical Body of Christ [Mystici Corporis Christi]* (Pauline Books and Media: 800-876-4463).

- Archbishop Daniel E. Pilarczyk, *The Parish: Where God's People Live* (Paulist Press: 800-218-1903).

SEVENTEEN

Can We Find the Time to Love Our Neighbor?

When it comes to social action, we find ourselves in a predicament. Jesus' command to love our neighbor compels us to be concerned for others. And the Church tells us we should have a preferential option for the poor—for those involuntarily caught in the jaws of poverty and injustice. But the enormity of contemporary social problems overwhelms us. We feel responsible for the great needs we see, yet we seem to be paralyzed and unable to meet them. We want to do something, but don't even know where to begin.

Statistics, I think, are the culprit. They bewilder us. Daily we are deluged with numbers that apprise us of society's problems. We flip on the T.V. news and learn that an estimated one-half million homeless people roam the streets of our cities; that one-and-a-half million babies were aborted last year; and that more than 320,000 have died of AIDS. We turn to the newspaper looking for better news only to discover that thirty-six million Americans live below the poverty level; that more than one hundred thousand women are raped every year; and that 20 percent of male high-school students carry weapons to school.[1] And so on. The sheer volume of statistical information deflates our hope of improving things. It neutralizes our eagerness to act.

A friend says to us, "In our city a thousand people are sleeping in doorways. What are *you* going to do about it?" Embarrassed, we clear our throats and mutter: "Nothing, I guess." Well, how could anything we attempted make even a dent in a need like that?

Statistics prevent us from taking any action because they are impersonal. We can easily decide not to do anything to serve a thousand faceless numbers. However, what if someone said to us, "Mary and her three-year-old, Joseph, are temporarily homeless. Could you take them in for a week until they are placed in public housing?"

A COMMITMENT TO SERVE THE LEAST

In the presence of suffering we cannot remain indifferent or passive. Before asking about the responsibility of others, believers listen to the voice of their Divine Master, who urges them to imitate the Good Samaritan. He dismounted in order to help the man who had been attacked by robbers on the road from Jerusalem to Jericho and spent his energy, time and money for him. First and foremost he offered him his compassionate heart (see Lk 10:30-37). Christians know they are called to put Christ's teaching into practice: "As you did it to the least of one of these my brethren, you did it to me" (Mt 25:40)....

Jesus came to proclaim the Gospel to the poor, so those who, aware of their limitations, feel the need of help from on high. Only the person who is poor in this sense, who is not proud or self-inflated, can understand that the wealth of light and grace received from God calls in turn for a free-offering of one's life for others.

For believers this is both an individual and a social duty. The example comes from the primitive Church, which gathered around the Apostles not only to hear their preaching and celebrate the Eucharist, but also to exercise charity with them. For this purpose they laid their possessions at the feet of the Apostles so that they could be distributed in turn to the poor.

We look into Joseph's winning eyes, big as giant black olives, and say, "You know, I do have a spare bedroom and little Joseph here could sleep on the cot my grandson uses when he visits."

When Jesus commanded us to love our neighbor as ourselves, he was speaking personally. He was talking to you and me about

---

The option or love of preference for the poor is a special form of primacy in the exercise of Christian charity, to which the whole tradition of the Church bears witness. It affects the life of each Christian inasmuch as he or she seeks to imitate the life of Christ, but it applies equally to our social responsibilities and hence to our manner of living, and to the logical decisions to be made concerning the ownership and use of goods....

The social message of the Gospel must not be considered a theory, but above all else a basis and a motivation for action. Inspired by this message, some of the first Christians distributed their goods to the poor, bearing witness to the fact that, despite different social origins, it was possible for people to live together in peace and harmony. Through the power of God, down the centuries men and women religious founded hospitals and shelters for the poor, confraternities as well as individual men and women of all states of life devoted themselves to the needy and to those on the margin of society—convinced as they were that Christ's words "As you did it to the least of one of these my brethren, you did it to me" were not intended to remain a pious wish but were meant to become a concrete life commitment.

Pope John Paul II, Address to the College of Cardinals, December 22, 1993[2]

the people on our street, in our car pool, in our classroom, on our job, at the grocery store and in our church. Flesh and blood people, not statistical indicators of social problems. The elderly lady across the street who has been recently diagnosed with Alzheimer's disease. The young associate at work who has been hospitalized with AIDS. The mother at church whose sixth child has Down's syndrome. The out-of-work brother who was the recent victim of downsizing. We must get past the smoke screen of statistics, and care for needy people face to face, one at a time.

I once heard an evangelist say that "love your neighbor" meant just that: love *one* neighbor. His point was that if every Christian took care of the needs of just one neighbor, the community of believers would cause significant improvement in society's problems. While I think this is a misinterpretation of Christ's command, I find it thought-provoking and encouraging. If we each improved the circumstances of one person, it would add up to a lot of betterment.

Another block to our obeying Jesus' love command is time. We don't think we have enough of it. We suppose that ordinary obligations and serving others are mutually exclusive. Either we fulfill our responsibilities to our family, our work and ourselves, or we cheat on these duties to help others. However, I don't think it has to be "either-or." We should be able to find some way to fit caring for others into our daily routines. Making time might just be a matter of scheduling ourselves a little more closely or creatively. Here are some examples of people like you and me who have built modest social action efforts into their lives:

- Grandpa David is retired. On Thursday afternoons after his golf game, he stops by a local public school to spend one hour reading to Sam, an at-risk kindergartner. David is thinking about taking Sam fishing with him every other Saturday morning.

- Over the past decade, Bridget and Will have taken into their family three pregnant teenagers. They supported these young women materially and spiritually, preparing them either to put their babies up for adoption or to care for them as single parents. Will and Bridget say the hospitality put some pressure on their family of five, but that everyone pitched in to make it work.

- Mike and Diane have three grade-school children, and both work full-time. One Saturday a month, the whole family volunteers for a two-hour stint at a downtown soup kitchen, dishing up food for the hungry.

- Marge has a disability that confines her to a wheelchair. Armed with her cell phone, she serves three mornings a week as Holy Redeemer Parish's contact with Love, Inc., a Christian relief agency. She refers people's needs to her church's volunteers.

- Drew was asked to work with Kairos, an ecumenical prison ministry. The commitment—one Tuesday evening a month for a year and a weekend retreat—meshed well with his busy schedule. He served for two and a half years before his duties at work made it impossible for him to continue.

Notice that in all these cases people found ways of loving their neighbor that fit in their normal pattern of life.

When Jesus commanded us to love our neighbors, I don't think he was limiting us to one-on-one service. Consider his own example. It would be a stretch, I think, to describe Christ as a social activist, but his behavior bore witness to social change and promoted it. For example, he associated freely with social outcasts. The Church has interpreted the Lord's teaching and example as giving the community of believers a responsibility to work for the transformation of society. We are to work peacefully for social, political and economic improvements that will benefit disadvantaged people. And we are to do it in a way that advances the gospel. Earthly improvements are important, but in the long run they are a poor substitute for eternal salvation.

For some, action for social justice means full-time work. Thousands of Catholics work for the state or the Church in jobs that are dedicated to fulfilling Christ's love command by bringing relief to the poor. Many others have retired, left jobs early or redefined their work situations to give them an opportunity to work for justice. And individuals and parishes have found other creative ways to have an impact on society. Consider these examples:

- Bob, a medical doctor, reshaped his practice twenty years ago so that he could offer the poor of his town a very low-cost clinic on three afternoons and evenings each week. As a result thousands of people are healthier.

- Ferdi Mahfood left his lucrative business as an international merchant to found Food for the Poor. Every year that remarkable organization provides ministries in Haiti and Jamaica with millions of dollars' worth of food and other necessary items.

- A large parish in Clearwater, Florida, and numerous other parishes around the country, tithe their offerings to the poor, often through organizations like Food for the Poor.

- Every year St. Mary Magdalen Parish in Altamonte Springs, Florida, constructs Habitat for Humanity houses. Their actions both shelter those who need homes and build a bridge across denominational divides within the Christian community, as the beneficiaries are frequently members of Protestant churches. Numerous parishes in central Florida and throughout the United States are undertaking similar actions.

- When several new abortion clinics opened in their city, Greg and Leah organized a team of their friends who volunteered many hours to open a pregnancy counseling center as an alternative. Among many activities, the group raised money, got training for counselors, received state certification, rented and equipped a store front, purchased materials and so on. After several years they were able to transform it into a professionally administered agency.

Most of us are not called in the same way as Dr. Bob, Ferdi Mahfood or Greg and Leah. But we are all called to look for ways to obey Jesus' command to love our neighbor. Maybe if I rearrange a few things, I could free up one Saturday morning a month. Where do you think you might find some time to serve a neighbor?

FOR REFLECTION AND DISCUSSION

1. What responsibility does a Christian have toward the poor?

2. What obstacles do contemporary Christians face in trying to obey the command to love our neighbor? What can I do to overcome these blocks in my life?

3. What do you think it means to have a "preferential option for the poor"?

4. In what ways do you think social action can help make people aware of the gospel of salvation?

5. What can I do differently to fit some form of social outreach into my life?

A C T I O N   I D E A S

1. Look for some way to reach out to disadvantaged people once during Lent or the Easter season. Involve your family or a few friends in the activity. Do it every year, making it a regular part of your celebration of that Christian season.

2. Find out what your parish does in the area of service to the poor. Review your schedule and, if possible, volunteer to work in a parish-based social action program. Be sure that you limit yourself to a reasonable amount of time so that you can keep the commitment. Put a term on your involvement, which will allow you to evaluate and adjust your commitment if necessary.

3. If you are not already making some monetary contribution to the poor, review your finances to determine what you might be able to do. Find a charitable organization whose goals you like and make a personal decision to contribute a specific amount each month for a year. At the end of the year, review what you have done. If possible, do it again.

R E A D   M E !

- Archbishop Daniel E. Pilarczyk, *Bringing Forth Justice: Basics for Christians* (Paulist Press: 800-218-1903).

- Vatican Council II, *Pastoral Constitution on the Church in the Modern World [Gaudium et Spes]* (Pauline Books & Media: 800-876-4463) is the fundamental Catholic document on social action.

Putting Your Faith Into Practice

Now you've done it! You have read a book on how to practice the Catholic faith. So, my question to you is: What are you going to do about it? For like all authors of practical books, my aim in writing is twofold—not only to expand your understanding, but to get you to act on what you have learned. Of course, you don't have to do anything in response to *Being Catholic Today,* but that would be like reading a book on word processing and never touching a computer keyboard. Or a book on cooking and never even boiling water. Or a book on golf and never swinging a club.

Your purpose in picking up this book will help you decide what you should do as your "take-away" from reading it.

- If you are thinking about becoming Catholic, I suggest that you visit a parish in your neighborhood, and begin attending an inquirer's class. Let this book be a resource for your investigation.

- You may be participating in the Rite of Christian Initiation for Adults (RCIA). You may consult *Being Catholic Today* as a support for making your faith decisions during the process.

- If you are hoping to fill up gaps in your Catholic formation, let this book be your guide. Identify the areas where you feel the greatest need and review the chapters that seem to apply most to your situation. I advise you to tackle just one thing at a time.

- Are you an active Catholic looking for a refresher course? You may use *Being Catholic Today* to choose one thing you could do differently to revitalize an element in your faith life you judge needs renewal.

Here I am urging you to undertake a lot of "doing," but I don't want to cover up this fundamental truth of being Catholic: God is primarily the doer, and we are the object of his graces. He is the giver, we the receiver. He is the lover and we the beloved. Practicing the faith affects everything in our lives, and it involves us in a certain amount of activity. But remember, everything we do is a response to God. The most appropriate expression of our Catholic faith is surrendering to him.

NOTES

ONE
What Does It Mean to Be "Catholic"?

1. Frank Sheed, *Theology for Beginners* (Ann Arbor, Mich.: Servant, 1982), 110.
2. Robert Bellarmine, cited in *Handbook for Today's Catholic* (Ligouri, Mo.: Liguori, 1978), 28.
3. See *Catechism of the Catholic Church* (#888–92).
4. "Look Beyond," by Darryl Ducote, copyright ©1969 by F.E.L. Publications, Ltd.

TWO
When Catholics Come of Age

1. *Tertio Millennio Adveniente* (November 14, 1994), 7.
2. Fr. Edward O'Connor, *The Catholic Vision* (Huntington, Ind.: Our Sunday Visitor, 1992), 396.

SIX
Living Through the Year With Christ

1. *Constitution on the Sacred Liturgy [Sacrosanctum Concilium]*, 102.

SEVEN
Spend Time With the Lord

1. *The Autobiography of St. Teresa of Avila*, tr. E. Allison Peers (Garden City, N.Y..: Image Books, 1960), 127–28.

TEN

Meet the Holy Spirit, the Worker

1. "Veni Sancte Spiritus," tr. Rev. Dr. John Webster Grant in *The Hymn Book of the Anglican Church of Canada and the United Church of Canada,* © 1971. Used by permission.

ELEVEN

Doing the Right Thing

1. C.S. Lewis, *Mere Christianity* (New York: Collier, 1952), 160–66.

FIFTEEN

Making Friends for Christ and the Church

1. *Mission of the Redeemer [Redemptoris Missio],* no. 3.

SEVENTEEN

Can We Find the Time to Love Our Neighbor?

1. Sources: *Information Plus* (1996) *AIDS; Crime; Homeless in America; Statistical Abstract of the United States,* 1997; *World Almanac,* 1997.
2. Address to the College of Cardinals, December 22, 1993; and *On the Hundredth Anniversary of Rerum Novarum (Centesimus Annus),* no. 57.

RECOMMENDED RESOURCES

Catechism of the Catholic Church (available from several publishers).

Vatican Council II Documents (all are published by Pauline Books & Media: 800-876-4463).

Constitution on the Sacred Liturgy [Sacrosanctum Concilium].
Decree on the Apostolate of the Laity [Apostolicam Actuositatem].
Dogmatic Constitution on the Church [Lumen Gentium].
Dogmatic Constitution on Divine Revelation [Dei Verbum].
Pastoral Constitution on the Church in the Modern World [Gaudium et Spes].

Encyclical Letters (all are available from Pauline Books & Media: 800-876-4463).

Evangelization in the Modern World [Evangelii Nuntiandi], encyclical letter of Pope Paul VI.
The Mission of the Redeemer [Redemptoris Missio], encyclical letter of Pope John Paul II.
On the Mystical Body of Christ [Mystici Corporis Christi], encyclical letter of Pope Pius XI.

Books and Magazines
Peg Bowman, *At Home with the Sacraments: Reconciliation.* (Twenty-Third Publications: 800-321-0411).
Catechism of the Catholic Church (Our Sunday Visitor: 800-348-2440).
Catholic Parent magazine (Our Sunday Visitor: 800-348-2440).
The Catholic Prayer Book (Servant Publications: 734-677-6490).
The Collegeville Bible Commentary (Liturgical Press: 800-858-5450).
J. Augustine DiNoia, O.P., et al., *The Love That Never Ends: A Key to the*
Mitch Finley, *The Joy of Being Catholic* (Crossroad: 212-532-3650).
Bert Ghezzi, *50 Ways to Tap the Power of the Sacraments* (Our Sunday Visitor: 800-348-2440).
_____, *Guiltless Catholic Parenting* (Servant Publications: 734-677-6490).

_____, *Keeping Your Kids Catholic* (Servant Publications: 734-677-6490).

_____, *Miracles of the Saints: True Stories of Lives Touched by the Supernatural* (Zondervan: 800-727-3480).

_____, *Sharing Your Faith: A User's Guide to Evangelization* (Our Sunday Visitor: 800-348-2440).

God's Word Today (Catholic Digest: 800-335-7771).

Thomas Green, S.J., *Opening to God: A Personal Guide to Prayer for Today* (Ave Maria: 800-282-1865).

Handbook for Today's Catholic (Liguori: 314-464-2500).

John Hardon, S.J., *The Faith* (Servant Publications: 734-677-6490).

Henry Libersat, *A Catholic Confession of Faith* (Pauline Books & Media: 800-876-4463).

George Martin, *Reading Scripture as the Word of God* (Servant Publications: 734-677-6490).

Alfred McBride, O. Praem., *Essentials of the Faith* (Our Sunday Visitor: 800-348-2440).

LaVonne Neff, *Breakfast With the Saints* (Servant: 734-677-6490).

New Covenant (Our Sunday Visitor: 800-348-2440).

Edward O'Connor, C.S.C., *The Catholic Vision* (Our Sunday Visitor: 800-348-2440).

Mitch Pacwa, S.J., *Father Forgive Me, For I Am Frustrated* (Servant Publications: 734-677-6490).

Archbishop Daniel E. Pilarczyk, *The Parish: Where God's People Live* (Paulist Press: 800-218-1903).

_____, *Understanding the Mass* (Our Sunday Visitor: 800-348-2440).

Alan Schreck, *Basics of the Faith* (Servant Publications: 734-677-6490).

_____, *Catholic & Christian* (Servant Publications: 734-677-6490).

_____, *Hearts Aflame: The Holy Spirit at the Heart of Christian Life Today* (Servant: 734-677-6490).

Frank Sheed, *Theology for Beginners* (Servant Publications: 734-677-6490).